Hands on Phonics

Liz Webster
Sue Reed

Acknowledgements

Liz Webster, head teacher of Aldingbourne Primary School and her deputy head teacher, Sue Reed, would like to thank all the children and staff of their school for their enthusiasm, hard work and cooperation in the making of this book. They would like especially to thank Wendy Davies for her hard work and dedication, particularly during some very late nights at school! Sue Reed would like to express a special thanks to her husband Ollie for his never-ending patience and support. Finally they would like to thank Steve Forest, the photographer, for always being so helpful and easy to work with. The authors and publishers would like to say a big thanks to everybody.

Connect Four (page 24)

Published by Collins, An imprint of HarperCollins*Publishers*
77 – 85 Fulham Palace Road, Hammersmith, London, W6 8JB

Browse the complete Collins catalogue at
www.collinseducation.com

© HarperCollins*Publishers* Limited 2011
Previously published in 2008 by Folens
First published in 2008 by Belair Publications

10 9 8 7 6 5 4 3 2

ISBN-13 978-0-00-743939-3

Liz Webster and Sue Reed assert their moral rights to be identified as the authors of this work

British Library Cataloguing in Publication Data
A Catalogue record for this publication is available from the British Library

Every effort has been made to trace copyright holders and to obtain their permission for the use of copyright material. The authors and publishers will gladly receive any information enabling them to rectify any error or omission in subsequent editions.

Commissioning Editor: Zöe Parish   Editors: Joanne Murray
Cover design: Mount Deluxe   Page layout: Barbara Linton
Photography: Steve Forrest

Printed and bound by Printing Express Limited, Hong Kong

MIX
Paper from
responsible sources

FSC
www.fsc.org   FSC C007454

Contents

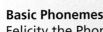
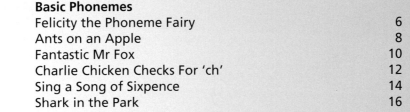

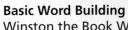

Introduction

Welcome to *Hands on Phonics*. Over recent years the importance of high quality phonics teaching has been highlighted as being fundamental to children's reading and writing.

This book aims to show how phonics can be taught and displayed through a creative, dynamic and, above all, FUN approach. Most schools will already have a synthetic phonics programme that they follow. The ideas in this book will complement any phonics programme and enhance both the teaching for learning and the classroom environment through its stimulating approach.

What Do We Mean By Phonics?

Phonics are the tools by which children learn to read and write. To learn to read and write the children need to learn five basic skills. They need to:

1. Learn the phonemes.
2. Learn to form their letters.
3. Learn to identify and blend phonemes together for reading.
4. Learn to identify and segment phonemes for spelling.
5. Learn to read and spell irregular words.

Learning the Phonemes

You should aim to teach the basic phonemes as quickly and comprehensively as possible so that children can begin to read and write independently earlier.

The main phonemes of English should be taught alongside the names of the letters.

These basic phonemes are:

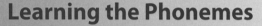

s a t p i n m d g o c k e u r h b f l j v w x y z qu ch sh th ng ai ee igh oa oo ar or er ou oi

For each phoneme you can invent an action to help the children remember it. Every day some time should be spent practising the phonemes and actions and hearing the phonemes in words. As the letter names are taught, the children could take them home on flashcards to practice the phoneme associated with the letter name.

The phonemes should not be introduced in alphabetical order; one way is shown in the order above. The first few phonemes have deliberately been chosen because when put together they make simple three-letter words.

Phonemes with more than one way of being written are taught first in one form only, for example, the phoneme 'ai' (rain) is introduced first, with the alternatives 'ay' (day) and 'a-e' (cake) being taught later.

Letter Formation

It is very important that alongside their phonics teaching, children are taught to form their letters correctly. This begins with learning to hold a pencil. If the grip starts incorrectly it is very difficult to get it right later on. Children will then begin to practice how to form each letter correctly; starting in the right place and moving their pencil in the right direction. Letters could be taught with a joining tail at the end to make it easier to transfer into joined writing once they are ready.

Blending Phonemes Together for Reading

Blending is the process of saying the phonemes in a word and then running them together to read the word, for example, 'c-a-t, cat'. It is a technique that children need to learn, and it improves with practice. To help children practise it is helpful to reinforce the idea that the phonemes must be said quickly to hear the word, for example, 'b-u-s'. It is also easier if the first phoneme is said slightly louder, for example, '**b**-u-s'.

Identifying Phonemes in Words

To begin to write independently children need to be able to hear and segment the phonemes in words and to write the letters for these phonemes. The activities in this book provide numerous opportunities for children to practise listening for the phonemes and writing down the letters for these phonemes. This is the first step towards becoming an independent writer.

Tricky Words

Some words cannot be spelled by listening for the phonemes in them. These are irregular 'tricky words' and have to be learnt. As children become more fluent at reading and writing, they will need to be taught how to cope with many irregular words.

Throughout the book we have demonstrated that the most effective phonics lessons are practical and exciting for the children. Each chapter offers a range of stimulating and original ideas that we use in our classrooms – so we know they work! The chapters move from the very early stages of phonics teaching in which the basic phonemes are taught, through to the stage where children are exploring and experimenting within the world of words once they are secure in their phonetic knowledge. At each stage the children should be engaged in lively lessons in which fun and exciting games reinforce their learning and help them to develop into keen young readers and writers.

Every theme in this book follows the same basic structure by including a whole-class starter, practical activities, ideas for display and cross-curricular links.

Whole-class Starter:

This is the starting point for each theme and to engage and stimulate the children it must be exciting, meaningful and relevant. Teaching strategies include teacher in role, children working with a 'talk partner' to discuss ideas, lively games and visual props, including the use of an interactive whiteboard.

Practical Activities:

This part of the lesson reinforces the learning that has taken place during the whole-class starter session and must be equally exciting. We have included many practical ideas for different kinds of games, as well as ideas for how to record work in an imaginative way.

Display Ideas:

By displaying phonics work within the school environment we are not only raising the profile of phonics teaching as a fun and friendly subject, but also giving children opportunities for further reading and writing through interacting with the display.

Cross-curricular Links:

We have highlighted ways in which links can be made between phonics and other curriculum areas to help learning become more relevant and meaningful for young children.

So remember … phonics is a fun and rewarding part of the curriculum for both child and teacher, and if taught imaginatively can make a real difference to every child's ability to develop into a reader and writer.

So … get funky with your phonics!

Liz Webster and Sue Reed

Felicity the Phoneme Fairy

Whole-class Starter

- Enter the class in role as Felicity the Phoneme Fairy. Explain to the children that you have been sent to teach them all about phonemes. Explain to the children what a phoneme is. Show them a variety of letters from a bag and say the corresponding phoneme. Model the pure sound of the phoneme to the children. In the bag suddenly notice some 'pesky numbers'. Act horrified and ask the children to sort the letters from the numbers together. Each time a letter is picked out tell them the corresponding phoneme and place it on the board. Put the 'pesky numbers' in the bin.

- Play 'Find a Phoneme'. Using the letters that have been placed on the board, ask the children to call out the correct phoneme as you point to them with a magic wand. To make this more exciting, challenge the children to get quicker and include a corresponding word that begins with the phoneme.

- Play 'Speed Phonemes'. Pick six of the most basic phonemes, for example, 's', 'a', 't', 'p', 'i' and 'n'. Show the children these letters on either the interactive whiteboard or giant flashcards. The flashcards should also include a picture as well as a grapheme. Challenge the children to say the phonemes as quickly as they can as you show them one card at a time. This activity should be done daily and new phonemes added each day. Once again, an extension to this activity would be to think of words that begin with this phoneme.

Focus of Learning

- To understand that a phoneme is a single unit of sound and each phoneme is represented by a grapheme

Practical Activities

- Play 'Sieve for Phonemes'. Using plastic letters hide a selection of letters in sand. Make a set of picture cards that correspond with the hidden letters. The children take it in turns to pick a picture card and then together they sieve in the sand to try and find the corresponding phoneme. The children should be encouraged to repeatedly say the phoneme as they sieve for the plastic letters.

- Play 'Search for Phonemes'. Make a selection of star-shaped cards with a picture on the back. Hide the cards around the classroom or school. Give each child a whiteboard. The children search for the stars and when they find a star they look at the picture and identify the initial phoneme. The children practise saying the phoneme. The children should then be encouraged to write the initial phoneme on their whiteboard. This could be extended by encouraging them to write the corresponding word or phrase.

- Play 'Find the Phoneme'. Make a set of bingo boards with different phonemes on each of them. Make a set of corresponding picture cards and pop them in a box. The children take it in turns to pick a picture card. The object of the game is to try and find the phoneme on the board that matches the picture and cover it with a counter. The child who covers all their phonemes wins the game.

Display Ideas

- Draw and chalk pastel Felicity the Phoneme Fairy. Ask the children to draw their own picture of a phoneme. Place the pictures with the corresponding phonemes around Felicity. This can be used as a teaching aid.

- Ask the children to collage different giant-sized letters using different textures. For example, sandpaper, corrugated card, bubble wrap etc. These letters could be used for an interactive display activity in which children are blindfolded, given a phoneme and through touch try and identify the phoneme.

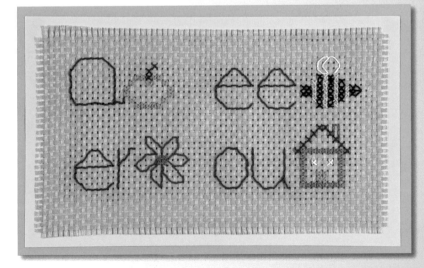

Cross-curricular Links

- **ART** – Create a class Victorian sampler using binca material and a choice of threads. Invite the children to sew a phoneme and corresponding picture.

- **LITERACY** – Ask the children to create their own alphabet zigzag book. Encourage the children to create their own phrases for a phoneme of their choice and illustrate them accordingly.

- **HISTORY/GEOGRAPHY** – Look at and discuss alphabets from around the world or from past times. For example, the Greek alphabet, the Chinese alphabet, Braille etc.

Ants on an Apple

Whole-class Starter

Focus of Learning

- To learn to say, recognise and write the phoneme 'a'

- Enter the class with a basket full of objects. Take out one object at a time and say the word, emphasising the initial phoneme (all the objects should begin with the phoneme 'a'). Ask the children what they notice about the objects. Pick each object up at a time and ask the children to repeat the word. For example, "aaa apple" or "aaa ambulance". Ask the children to all say the 'a' phoneme and model the shape their mouths should be. Ask them to say it in a quiet voice, noisy voice, sad voice, opera voice etc.

- Show the children a flashcard with a picture relating to the phoneme 'a'. For example, ants on an apple and the grapheme 'a'. The picture card should also have just the grapheme 'a' on the reverse side. Show the children the side with the picture and ask them to say "Ants on an apple aaa". Show the children the reverse and ask them to say "aaa". Repeat several times. Hide the card behind your back and show the children different sides and encourage the children to respond. Using the side with just the grapheme, trace it with your finger modelling the correct grapheme formation. Ask the children to write the grapheme in the air, on a partner's back and on their hand whilst saying "Ants on an apple aaa".

- On the interactive whiteboard use a multimedia package to create a presentation in which a range of graphemes appear on the screen at varying speeds and in various ways. The presentation should include lots and lots of 'a' graphemes as well as other random graphemes. The children watch the presentation and every time an 'a' grapheme appears they say the phoneme "aaa". This could be extended to writing the grapheme on whiteboards.

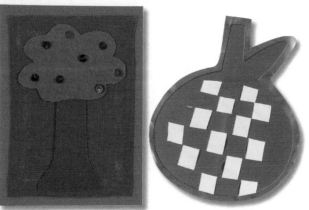

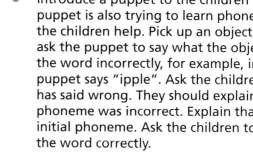

- Introduce a puppet to the children and explain that the puppet is also trying to learn phonemes and suggest that the children help. Pick up an object from a basket and ask the puppet to say what the object is. The puppet says the word incorrectly, for example, instead of "apple" the puppet says "ipple". Ask the children what the puppet has said wrong. They should explain that the initial phoneme was incorrect. Explain that this is called the initial phoneme. Ask the children to help the puppet say the word correctly.

Practical Activities

- Play 'Phoneme Fun'. Using either a set of large picture flashcards or pictures on the interactive whiteboard ask the children to stand up. Show a picture on the flashcard and if it begins with the phoneme 'a' the children must call out the name of the object. For example, 'apple', 'arrow', 'ambulance'. If a picture is shown that does not begin with the phoneme 'a' and a child shouts out that object the child must sit down and is out of the game. The child who remains standing at the end wins the game.

- Play 'Apple Picking'. Make a set of apple tree laminated boards (each tree needs at least six apples). Make a set of individual small apples with a picture on the back. Some of the pictures need to begin with the phoneme 'a' and some need to begin with other phonemes. Give each child in the group an apple board. Place the small apples in a bag or on an apple tree (made from wood or on the wall). Each child in the group takes it in turn to pick an apple and look at the picture. If the apple has a picture of something that begins with the letter 'a' they can cover up an apple on their apple tree. If it does not have a picture of an 'a' they put it back. The object of the game is to cover all the apples on the board.

- Cut out a giant-sized apple. Gather together a selection of pens, pencils, crayons, oil pastels; all red and green shades. Show the children how to correctly form the grapheme 'a'. Explain that they are going to fill the large apple with different coloured graphemes 'a'. Roll a dice and whatever number it lands on the children write that amount of graphemes 'a' on the apple. For example, if they roll a six they each write six graphemes 'a' on the apple. After each roll of the dice the children change their writing tool. This activity could be repeated, giving each child their own apple.

Display Ideas

- Using tissue paper and card make a giant 3D apple tree.

- Colour mix shades of red and green paint on large apple-shaped paper.

- Draw giant-sized ants using chalk pastels.

- Ask the children to write large words that begin with the grapheme 'a'.

- Ask the children to draw pictures of objects that begin with the grapheme 'a', place onto the giant apples and hang them from the apple tree.

Cross-curricular Links

- **ART** – Apple weave using strips of green and red paper or fabric.
  Sew an apple tree onto blue felt or hessian fabric using thick thread.
  Stick on red sequins to depict apples on a tree.

  Using polystyrene tiles, printing inks and a roller create a printing tile in the shape of an apple. Print red apples onto a green background and green apples onto a red background. Stick together to create a collage.

- **MATHS** – Taste a variety of different apples. Ask the children to choose their favourite and show the results as a pictogram or bar graph.

- **PSHCE** – Retell the story of *Johnny Appleseed* from *Look and Find Heroes and Legends* by Jerry Tiritilli (Publications International). Discuss his actions and why he behaved in this way.

Fantastic Mr Fox

Whole-class Starter

- Read the story *Fantastic Mr Fox* by Roald Dahl and Quentin Blake (Puffin Books). Discuss the title of the book and ask the children what they notice about it. Show them the 'f' phoneme on a flashcard.

- Using a home DVD recorder, dress up as Mr Fox and record a message to play to the children. Explain that he is really sad because the nasty farmers, Boggis, Bunce and Bean, keep trying to shoot him and he can't understand why. He is not a fierce fox but a friendly fantastic fox and if they got to know him they would really like him. He should talk to the children about all the things he does that make him fantastic, using objects that begin with the phoneme 'f'. For example, he has a picture of his **f**amily and he loves his **f**our children. He plays **f**ootball and likes to keep **f**it. He spends time **f**ishing and making **f**airy cakes with his children. He is good at tunnelling under **f**ences and he has lots of **f**riends including **f**ire-**f**ighter **F**red. He explains that he is fantastically clever because all the things he does begin with the phoneme 'f'. Mr Fox says goodbye to the children and he asks them to see if they can think of any more words that begin with the phoneme 'f'.

- After watching the recording, ask the children to recall what Mr Fox was good at. Encourage the children to say the words emphasising the 'f' phoneme. Show them different objects or pictures that begin with the phoneme 'f' and ask the children to say the 'f' phoneme in a quiet voice, loud voice, witch's voice, giant's voice etc.

- Show the children the grapheme 'f' and show them that the shape looks just like Mr Fox. Explain that when you write the 'f' grapheme you start at the top of Mr Fox's 'head' and work down to his 'tail'. You then take your pencil away and add his 'arms'. Ask the children to practise writing the grapheme 'f' in the air, on a partner's back, on their hand and on a whiteboard.

Focus of Learning

- To learn to say, recognise and write the phoneme 'f'

Practical Activities

- Make each child in the group a playing board with pictures of Mr Fox on it. In the middle of the table place a bag full of graphemes that the children can handle. Some of the graphemes should be 'f' graphemes and the others should be an assortment of other graphemes. The children should take it in turns to pull a grapheme out of the bag. If the grapheme is an 'f' they can put it on one of their foxes and cover it up. The first player to cover all of their foxes is the winner.

- Play 'I Spy an "f"'. Give each child a whiteboard and a pen. Ask them to visit different parts of the school and look for things that begin with the phoneme 'f'. If they discover something that begins with 'f' they must write the grapheme on their whiteboard. An extension to this activity could be to ask children to segment the whole word into phonemes to spell it.

- Play 'Fantastic Mr Fox'. In a group of about eight children choose three children to be the farmers Boggis, Bunce and Bean. These children could wear farmers' hats and wellies. Make a set of large laminated chicken pictures. On the reverse side stick a picture of either something that begins with 'f' or something that does not. The children who are not the farmers are Fantastic Mr Foxes and could wear a tag rugby belt as a tail. The object of the game is for the Mr Fox children to collect as many 'f' chickens as they can. If they get tagged by one of the farmers they must put all their chickens back. At the end of the game discuss the pictures the children have collected and whether their choices were correct.

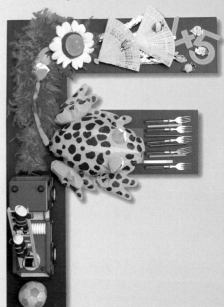

Display Ideas

- Paint and collage a large picture of Mr Fox and his three worst enemies, Boggis, Bunce and Bean.

  - Ask the children to draw and watercolour, in the style of Quentin Blake, their own picture of Mr Fox performing an action related to the phoneme 'f'. For example Mr Fox playing football, Mr Fox baking fairy cakes etc.

  - Make an 'f' sculpture. Ask each child in the class to bring an object from home that begins with the phoneme 'f'. Challenge the children to use the objects to make a sculpture of something that begins with the phoneme 'f'. Photograph the sculpture.

  - Print an 'f'. Using different printing tools and objects ask the children to print 'f' graphemes using different tools, techniques and colours. These could be used to make a giant class 'f' or as individual pictures.

Cross-curricular Links

- **LITERACY** – Ask the children to write a letter to Boggis, Bunce and Bean explaining that they should not shoot Mr Fox because he really is fantastic.
  Look at alliteration in relation to children's names, for example, 'Fantastic Mr Fox', 'Super Smiley Sophie', 'Racing Running Roger'.

- **SCIENCE** – Discuss the food chain with the children. For example, where does a fox come in the food chain? Is a fox a predator or prey or both?

- **PSHCE** – Discuss with the children the concept of being kind and caring to those around us. Read the book *The Friendly Fox* by Jenny Koralek and Beverley Gooding (Egmont Children's Books).

Charlie Chicken Checks For 'ch'

Whole-class Starter

Focus of Learning

- To learn to say, recognise and write the phoneme 'ch'

- Introduce a chicken puppet to the class. Explain that its name is Charlie Chicken and ask the class if they notice anything about its name. Explain that he is a very clever chicken because he is able to check for 'ch' diagraphs in any word. He has come today to challenge the children to check for 'ch' in words. Show the children a 'ch' diagraph and explain that when a 'c' and an 'h' come together they make a new phoneme that is a 'ch'. Show the children several examples such as 'chair', 'chest', 'cheese', 'chicken' etc.

- Play 'Check for "ch"'. Make a set of picture and word cards that have some words with a 'ch' and some without. Make enough cards for each child in the class. Sit the children in a circle and place a 'ch' chest and a rubbish bin in the middle. Give each child a card and ask them to take it in turns to decide whether their card is a 'ch' word and belongs in the 'ch' chest or a word without a 'ch' and belongs in the rubbish bin. Play some music, for example, 'Chitty Chitty Bang Bang', and ask the children to sensibly put their card in either the chest or rubbish bin.

- Play 'Chase the "ch"'. You will need a large outside space or hall and a chequered flag. Make a set of ten laminated 'ch' cards and hide them around the outside space or hall. Make a selection of picture cards; some 'ch' words and some not (you will need to make enough cards for each child). Give each child a card and when you wave the chequered flag the children must decide if they need to find a 'ch' card or not. If they do not need a 'ch' card they must make their way to the 'pit stop' (an area made with cones). If they do need a 'ch' they must chase around the area and try to find a 'ch' card. Wave the chequered flag after a set time and the chase stops. Any child who has been successful goes to the 'pit stop' and is still in the game. Any child who has been unsuccessful or incorrect in their decision is out of the game. The winner of the game is the child who stays in the game the longest.

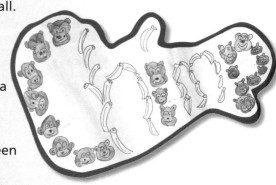

Practical Activities

- Play 'Ch, Ch, Chicken'. Make a set of bingo-style chequered boards. On each square place a picture of a 'ch' word. Make a six spinner or a dice with four 'ch' sections and two sections with chickens on. The children take it in turns to spin the spinner or roll the dice. If it lands on a 'ch' the child can cover one of their 'ch' words on their bingo board. If it lands on a chicken each child must correctly write on a whiteboard the 'ch' words they have already covered on their board. If they are incorrect they must remove the appropriate counter. The object of the game is to cover all the 'ch' words on their board.

- Play 'Challenge Charlie Chicken'. Make a Charlie Chicken hat, badge or use the Charlie Chicken puppet. You will also need to make a giant-sized 'ch' wordsearch on the interactive whiteboard or using squared paper. Make a set of clues that correspond to the 'ch' words on the giant wordsearch. In a small group the children take it in turns to wear the chicken hat, badge or puppet. Read out a clue and the child must identify the 'ch' word and find it on the wordsearch. Each child has one minute to find as many 'ch' words as they can.

- Play 'Chipping Chickens'. You will need chipping nets, a tri-golf club and several tri-golf balls. To play this game you will need a large space. Make lots of laminated chickens, ensuring they are large enough for 'ch' words to be written on them. Number the chipping nets 'one', 'two', 'three' and 'four'. The children take it in turns to chip a ball into one of the nets. If a child correctly chips a ball into a net, they must collect that amount of chickens and write a 'ch' word on each one. For example, if a child chips a ball into the net labelled 'three' the child takes three chickens and must write a 'ch' word correctly on each one. The object of the game is to collect as many chickens as possible.

Display Ideas

- Paint and collage a large Charlie Chicken.

- Use black and white squared paper to create a chequered board effect.

- Draw and paint large pictures of 'ch' words.

Cross-curricular Links

- **GEOGRAPHY** – Go on a 'ch' walk around the school or local area. Use a plan of the school to mark the location of 'ch' objects.

- **DESIGN & TECHNOLOGY** – Make a Charlie Chicken puppet.

- **ART** – Use chalk pastels to draw and colour pictures of Charlie Chicken.

- **ART & LITERACY** – Ask each child to draw a black and white 'ch' picture. Collage the pictures together. Use the finished picture as an 'I Spy' game or a literacy activity. Ask the children to write simple sentences about what they can see. For example, 'I can see a church' or 'I can see a chunky chair'.

Sing a Song of Sixpence

Whole-class Starter

- Share the poem 'Sing a Song of Sixpence' with the children from the book *A Stitch in Rhyme: Nursery Rhymes with Embroideries* by Belinda Downes (Mammoth). Explain to the children that you are reading this poem because it has got lots of words in it that end in 'ng'. Show the children one picture at a time and say the 'ng' word, emphasising the 'ng' phoneme. Ask the children to repeat the word after you have said it.

- Show the children how to write the phoneme 'ng' and discuss the fact that it has two letters but only makes one sound. Make a set of picture cards of 'ng' words. For example, 'sing', 'ring', 'king', 'swing', 'hang', 'bang' etc. Underneath the picture draw symbols to emphasise each phoneme. Draw a star symbol for phonemes with one letter and a long line for phonemes represented by two letters. For example, 'sing = ✳ ✳ ——'. Show the children a picture at a time and ask them to segment the words into phonemes. Repeat this several times. Give each child a whiteboard and pen and this time show them just the picture of an 'ng' word and ask them to write the word.

- Play 'Blackbird Pie'. Make a giant pie out of a box and paper. Make a set of blackbirds; some with an 'ng' picture on them and some with pictures that do not contain the 'ng' phoneme. Place the pie in front of the class. Make a washing line using string and pegs. Ask the children to take it in turns to pick a blackbird out of the pie. If it has an 'ng' picture on it they must hang it on the washing line; if it does not they must put the blackbird back in the pie.

Focus of Learning

- To learn to say, recognise and write the phoneme 'ng'

Practical Activities

- Play 'King's Pie'. Make a set of pie-shaped playing boards that have six 'ng' graphemes on them. Make a set of blackbirds with pictures on them that contain the 'ng' phoneme and some that do not. Place the pictures in a royal bag or crown. The children take it in turns to pick a blackbird. If it has a picture on that contains the 'ng' phoneme they can circle an 'ng' grapheme on their board using a dry-wipe marker pen. If it is not an 'ng' picture they put it back in the crown or bag and miss a go. The object is to circle all the 'ng' graphemes on their board.

- Play 'Is there an "ng" in the washing?' Make a set of laminated picture cards; some that contain an 'ng' phoneme and some that don't. Pin the pictures to different items of clothes and place the clothes in a washing basket. Using the washing line from the whole-class starter session ask each member of the group to choose a piece of clothing from the washing basket and place on the washing line. Ask the children to look carefully at the washing on the line and if any of the pictures contain an 'ng' phoneme they must write that word on a piece of card.

- Play 'Pie Pandemonium'. Make a set of circular pies that are cut into six pieces. Each member of the group will need a pie. Make a set of word cards that contain 'ng' words and a set that contain nonsense 'ng' words. For example, 'ongh', 'ngly', 'wang' etc. Sit each member of the group on a mat or in a hoop. Place the pie pieces in the middle of the room or large space. Place the words around the room on the wall. Make a dice that shows two king faces, two blackbirds and two 'ng' graphemes. Roll the dice and if it lands on the 'ng' the children race to find a correct 'ng' word. If they can read the word they are allowed to gather a piece of pie. If the dice lands on the king they must put all their pie pieces away. If the dice lands on a blackbird the children have 30 seconds to collect as many correct 'ng' words as they can find. The children are only allowed to gather a piece of pie if they can read the 'ng' word correctly. The object is to be the first person to build their pie.

- Play 'Sing a Song of Sixpence'. Use the blackbird pie from the whole-class starter session. Make a set of laminated blackbirds with 'ng' words written on them that have the 'ng' missing. Also make some blackbirds with a picture of a nose on and some blank blackbirds. The children take it in turns to place their hand in the pie and take out a blackbird. If they pick out a blackbird that has an 'ng' word they must write the 'ng' phoneme on the bird and then read the word correctly in order to keep it. If they select a blank blackbird they put it back and miss a go. If they pick a blackbird with a nose on they must put all their blackbirds back. The object is to collect as many blackbirds as they can.

Display Ideas

- Paint and collage a large fruit pie.

- Paint and collage blackbirds and place them popping out and around the pie.

- Ask the children to draw and oil pastel a selection of different pieces of washing.

- Draw and colour pictures of 'ng' words and place them on and around the blackbird pie.

Cross-curricular Links

- **DESIGN & TECHNOLOGY** – Ask the children to make and bake individual blackberry pies.

- **MATHS** – Invite the 'king' (you in role) from the story to visit the children and talk to them about counting money, the value of money and identifying money.

- **LITERACY** – Read and discuss other nursery rhymes with the children.

Shark in the Park

Whole-class Starter

Focus of Learning

- To learn to say, recognise and write the phoneme 'ar'

- Read the story *Shark in the Park* by Nick Sharratt (Corgi Children's Books). Discuss the title and ask the children what they notice about the words 'shark' and 'park'. The children will suggest lots of ideas such as they both rhyme, they end in the phoneme 'k', they both have an 'ar' phoneme in them etc. Show the children an 'ar' phoneme. Make a set of picture cards, some containing an 'ar' phoneme and some without. Use a hoop with an 'ar' in the middle. Give each child one of the picture cards and play the *Jaws* theme tune from *Jaws: Original Soundtrack* (John Williams). The children must come and either put their picture in the hoop if they think it contains an 'ar' phoneme or outside of the hoop if they think it doesn't.

- Using the spotlight tool on the interactive whiteboard or a large black spot, hide an 'ar' picture behind the spotlight or black spot and gradually reveal a small part of the picture. Ask the children to guess what the 'ar' picture is. Repeat several times and extend by asking the children to write the corresponding 'ar' word.

- Play 'Shark Attack'. Make a set of 'ar' word cards that have been 'attacked by a shark and have had the "ar" phoneme bitten off', for example, 'f**m' (farm). Make another set of word cards that have also been attacked by a shark and have had a phoneme bitten away but the missing phoneme is not an 'ar', for example, 'b**b' (bulb). Make a further set of cards with a picture of a shark on them. Organise the children into two teams. The object of the game is to collect the most 'ar' words. Put all of the cards face down in a paddling pool or blue mat to represent the pond. Each team takes it in turns to pick a word out of the 'pond'. If it is an 'ar' word they can keep it, if it isn't an 'ar' word they must miss a go. However, if they pick a shark card the team shouts "Shark attack!" and the opposite team has to put all their cards back in the pond.

Practical Activities

- Make a booklet for each child that has a circle cut in to every other page (a similar layout to the *Shark in the Park* book). Ask the children to draw 'ar' pictures in the booklet. The children write 'Timothy Pope, Timothy Pope, what can you see through your telescope?' on the front.

- Play 'Shark in the Park'. Make a selection of picture cards; some with 'ar' words and some without. Place a selection of hoops in a hall or an outside space. In the hoops place a card. In a small group make one child a shark (ask them to wear a bib with a picture on). The other children must move around the area but avoid touching a hoop. The shark swims gently amongst the children. Shout "Shark in the Park!" and at this point the children must find a hoop that has an 'ar' word in; if they stand in the hoop they are safe. If the shark catches somebody before they get into an 'ar' hoop they are out of the game. If a child selects an incorrect hoop they are also out of the game. The winner is the child who survives the shark attack.

- Play 'Timothy's Telescope'. Give each child a laminated scene in a similar style to the first page in the book including as many different 'ar' words as possible. Make a dice that has the numbers one, two, three, four and two sharks on it. The children take it in turns to roll the dice and whatever number they roll they may write that many 'ar' words on their boards under the corresponding pictures. If they roll a shark, however, they must rub off all their words! The winner is the child with the most 'ar' words at the end of the game.

- Play 'Shark and Show'. Make a selection of individual letters that when put together make an 'ar' word. Make a set of cards; some blank and some with a shark on. Give each child a selection of letters that make an 'ar' word, but place them face down so the children cannot see them. Place the other set of cards in a bag or box and each child takes it in turns to pick a card. If they pick a blank card nothing happens. If they pick a shark card the group must turn their letters over and try and make their 'ar' word as quickly as possible. The winner is the child who makes their 'ar' word correctly and shouts "Shark and Show!"

Display Ideas

- Make a red and green circular background in the style of the front cover of the book *Shark in the Park*.

- Collage and paint a picture of Timothy with his telescope.

- Collage and paint pictures of 'ar' words.

- Paint giant sharks and add 'ar' words coming out of each shark's mouth.

Cross-curricular Links

- **SCIENCE** – pond dipping: investigating real pond life. Investigate sharks and create a shark fact file.

Winston the Book Wolf

Whole-class Starter

Focus of Learning

- To learn to blend and segment phonemes in order to read words

- Read the book *Winston the Book Wolf* by Marni Mcgee and Ian Beck (Bloomsbury Publishing). Discuss how Rosie stopped Winston from eating words by teaching him to read. Discuss with the children the fact that Winston ate the words because they were so delicious and had the 'tingle factor'. Ask the children to think of their favourite word. Ask them to write down or draw a picture on a large stick-it of their favourite word. Place the stick-its on the board and discuss the selection of words.

- Use a 'Winston the Wolf' puppet as a stimulus. Explain that he has come to teach the class how to read words by sounding out phonemes. Use the puppet to explain to the class what a phoneme is and ask the class if they know any. Produce a bag or box full of phonemes and pull a phoneme out. Ask the children if they can identify the correct phoneme (repeat several times). Explain that learning phonemes is really clever but what is cleverer is that when phonemes are blended together they make words, and once you know words you can read!

- Play 'Winston's Words'. Using an interactive whiteboard create a multimedia presentation with a three-letter word made up of individual phonemes on each page. Include a picture of the three-letter word; hide the picture under a box. Use the Winston puppet to show the children how to read the word on the board by dragging the phonemes apart (segmenting), sounding each phoneme out individually and then moving them back together and blending them to create a word. Once this has been done reveal the picture to check if they are correct. This can be extended to include four-letter words.

Practical Activities

- Play 'Read and Roll'. Make a set of large A4 laminated lotto boards with six squares (number each square in the corner).On each square write a different three- or four-letter word, depending on the ability of the children. Each board should contain different words. Make a set of corresponding picture cards and place on a large whiteboard. The children take it in turns to roll a dice; whichever number they land on they read the word on that number square on their lotto board. If the word is read correctly they find the corresponding picture and cover up the word. The winner is the first child to cover all their words.

- Play 'Yummy Yummy Put a Word in my Tummy!' Using a postbox or large box turn it into Winston the Wolf by placing a picture of Winston or a wolf mask on the front. Make a coloured dice with a different colour for each player. Make a set of laminated cards in the same colours that are on the dice. On each set of cards write a three- or four-letter word. You will need at least ten of each colour. Place the cards face down in the middle of the table. Nominate each child in the group a colour (bibs or badges could be worn). The children take it in turns to roll the dice and whatever colour it lands on the child picks up one of their cards and attempts to read the word. If they are correct they place the word in Winston's mouth (postbox). The first person to get rid of all their cards is the winner.

- Play 'Where's Winston?' Prepare some cards with three- and four-letter words written on one side, and some corresponding cards with pictures of the words on them. Place all the cards face down on the table. The children take it in turns to pick up two cards at a time. If the child can read the card and has the corresponding picture they get to keep the cards. If they pick up two cards that don't correspond they place them back down on the table. If a child picks up a Winston the Wolf card they must place all their cards back in the middle of the table. The winner of the game is the child who collects the most matching cards.

Display Ideas

- Paint and collage a large Winston the Wolf.
- Ask the children to write words for display, split to show the phonemes.
- Paint or chalk pastel pictures that correspond with the words.

Cross-curricular Links

- **LITERACY** – Create a Winston the Wolf reading corner. Provide the children with costumes so they can re-enact the end of the story. For example, a wolf mask, dress and hat, an outfit for Rosie or the Librarian.

  Write a letter to Winston thanking him for his help in learning to read. Share with Winston their favourite book or words.

  Play 'I Spy'. Identify the nursery rhyme and fairy tale characters in the story. Ask the children if they can think of any more.

- **ICT** – Turn a programmable toy into Winston the Wolf. Place cards around the room and ask the children to send Winston the programmable toy to a word they can read.

- **PSHCE** – Discuss with the children Winston's behaviour in the beginning of the story. How did he behave? Was this the correct way to behave? Have they ever behaved badly? What did they do to make it better? What did Winston do to change his behaviour? Talk about treating others how they themselves would like to be treated. Ask the children to think of ways they should behave in school, at home, at the shops, in a library.

- **ART** – Make a wolf puppet to use in a role play area.

The Word Builder

Whole-class Starter

- In role as Bert the Builder, explain that Bert is not just a builder who builds houses but he also builds words. Bring in a wheelbarrow of plastic play bricks with phonemes on them. Check if the children know their phonemes by asking them to each pick a brick. Say the phoneme and together build a phoneme wall. Tell the children that if they know their phonemes they can not only learn to read but also write words. Out of a backpack pull out a picture of a three-letter word. Ask the children if they can think of the phonemes they would need to write this word. Ask one of the children to come and choose the correct bricks. Put the bricks together and show the children that when phonemes are blended together they make words.

- Give each child a whiteboard and a pen. Show the children a three- or four-letter word and ask the children to use the phoneme wall to help them write the words correctly. After the children have had a go, demonstrate using the phoneme wall how to make the words.

- Play 'Phoneme Fingers'. Say a phonetically regular word, for example, 'cat', 'ship' etc. The children must work out how many phonemes are in the word, for example, 'c – a – t = three', 'sh – i – p = three'. The children work out how many phonemes are in the word on their fingers and hide them behind their other hand. Say "ready, steady, reveal" and they all show their fingers, revealing how many phonemes they think are in the word. Ask the children to whisper all together the phonemes as they touch each finger.

Focus of Learning

- To learn to blend and segment phonemes in order to spell words

Practical Activities

- Play 'Word Building'. Use the set of phoneme bricks from the whole-class starter session and work with a small group. Make a set of picture cards to include regular words that include three, four or five phonemes. Ask a child to pull a picture card out of a bag or box and build that word using the correct phonemes. Ask all the children in the group to write the word on a whiteboard.

- Play 'The Building Battle'. Make a set of picture cards to include regular words that include three, four or five phonemes and place in a builder's hat in the middle of a table. Give each child a whiteboard and a selection of bricks from a construction kit. The object of the game is to build the highest wall. In order to do this the children pick a card out of the hat and on their whiteboard attempt to spell the word using their phonemes. However many phonemes the word contains, the child earns the corresponding number of bricks with which to build their wall.

- Play 'Building Bricks'. Give each child a zip wallet with a picture on the front. Inside each zip wallet put the letters that make the word on the picture. Ask the children to pick a bag and empty it and make the word using the letters. They then must roll a one–six dice and write the word that many times on a whiteboard.

- Play 'Wheel a Word'. Split children up so they are working in teams. Give each team a toy wheelbarrow and a set of building bricks that can be written on. Make a set of picture cards to include regular words that include three, four or five phonemes and place them inside a 'cement mixer', for example, a large bin. On a whistle, a member of each team must run with their wheelbarrow to the cement mixer and pick out a picture card. They then run to the pile of bricks and collect a brick and add it to their wheelbarrow along with the picture card. They must run back to their team and write the word on a brick. Once the word has been written the next person in the team may go. The winning team is the team who has 'built' the highest wall.

Display Ideas

- Colour mix bricks in different shades of red.
- Paint and collage Bert the Builder.
- Paint large diggers and add pictures.
- Ask children to write words that correspond to the pictures.

Cross-curricular Links

- **LITERACY** – Create a builder's café role play area. Include menus with pictures on that the builders can order. The waiters and waitresses then bring plates of phonemes that correspond to the picture ordered.

- **DANCE** – Create a dance to the song *Bob the Builder* from *Bob the Builder – the Album* (Little Demon). Use the idea of the people and machinery that work on a building site as a stimulus.

- **SCIENCE** – Investigate the materials needed to build a house and their properties.

The Cat in the Hat

Whole-class Starter

- Read the book *The Cat in the Hat* by Dr Seuss (HarperCollins). Explain that you are going to use this book to show them how to read and spell three-letter words. Show the children the front of the book and ask them if they can spot any words that have three letters and three phonemes. Identify the words 'cat' and 'hat'. Model to the children how the words have got three letters and three phonemes.

- Play 'Cat in the Hat'. Make a selection of three-letter word cards and place them in a big top hat. Pull out one card at a time and ask the children to read the words using the phonemes to help them. All the words need to be regular three-letter words, for example, 'sat', 'cat', 'sun', 'hen' etc.

- Go out of the classroom and into a large open place, for example the hall or playground. Take a selection of pictures of three-letter words. Place around the large space lots and lots of individual letters. Split the children into small groups and sit each group on a mat. Make each group a laminated top hat. On a given signal one child from each group collects a picture and then must race to collect the correct letters that make that three-letter word. For example, if a child picks the picture of a dog they must run and collect the letters 'd', 'o' and 'g'. They must place the letters on their top hat in the correct order. The group who completes this first receives a point.

22

Practical Activities

- Play 'Climb the Cat's Hat'. Make each child a playing board in the shape of the cat's hat. Make a selection of cards, some with pictures of three-letter words on them, some with mother coming home on them and some with the fish on them. Place the cards in a top hat. The children take it in turns to pick a card out of the hat. If they pick a card with a picture on they must write the three-letter word on the first stripe of the cat's hat. If they pick a picture of a fish they must rub out one word from their board and if they pick a picture of mother they must rub out all their words. The first child to have written a three-letter word on each part of the cat's hat and reach the top of the hat is the winner.

- Play 'Fun in a Box'. Make a collection of objects that represent three-letter words. For example, 'pen', 'pig', 'cat', 'peg' etc. Give each child a whiteboard and a pen. Tell the children you are going to open the box and show them the objects that are inside. As you take out each object say the word aloud and put the object on the table for the children to look at. When you have taken all the objects out of the box give the children one minute to look at the objects and then put them back in the box. The children must write down as many objects as they can remember on their whiteboard and the child with the most objects spelled correctly on their whiteboard is the winner.

- Make Cat in the Hat zigzag books in the shape of the cat's hat. On each page ask the children to draw and write a three-letter word.

Display Ideas

- Paint and collage a large Cat in the Hat.

- In pairs ask the children to paint a kite and to draw a picture of a three-letter word to place on the kite. On the tail of the kite ask the children to write the three letters that match the word.

- Ask the children to draw a picture of Cat in the Hat in different poses. Encourage them to look at shading.

- Give each child a piece of hat-shaped paper and ask them to choose either red or blue (colours used in the story) paint. Ask the children to colour mix shades of that colour to make a stripy blue or red hat.

Cross-curricular Links

- **LITERACY** – Ask the children to draw a large fish. Cut out a variety of orange scales and ask the children to write three-letter words on the scales and stick them on the fish.

- **MATHS** – Focus on counting in twos: two children, two things, two kites.

  Make a giant kite for the classroom and place multiples of two up the tail.

Connect Four

Whole-class Starter

- In role as a game show host, explain to the children that you have just got a new job presenting a show on the television called 'Connect Four', in which you challenge the contestants to connect four phonemes together to read and write words. Explain to the children that it involves different rounds. The first round is the 'reading round'. Prepare on the interactive whiteboard a selection of four-letter words with phonemes spread apart. Model how to blend phonemes together to read words. Then split the class into two teams and choose a contestant from each team to stand on the 'hot spots'. Reveal a word and the first contestant to blend the word successfully wins a point for their team. Reveal a picture of the correct word. Repeat a few times.

- Explain that round two is the 'spelling round'. This time give a contestant from each team a whiteboard and a pen. Show a picture on the interactive whiteboard and the first person to spell the word correctly is the winner. Reveal the correct spelling on the interactive whiteboard and model how to do it. Repeat a few times.

- Explain that round three is 'connect four'. On the interactive whiteboard show children a big connect four grid that is full of random letters. Underneath the grid is a smaller grid that has pictures representing four-letter words that have been covered up. Some of the spaces in the smaller grid should be left blank. Each team should be given a colour; either red or yellow. Pick a contestant to uncover one of the squares on the smaller grid. If it has a picture underneath they must find the letters that blend together to make that word on the bigger grid and click on them to colour them their team's colour. If the square that they uncover is blank they must miss a go. The other team then have a go and this continues until one team has four squares in a row.

- The final round is called 'connect together'. Prepare picture cards of four-letter words and individual letter cards that correspond with the pictures. Give each child either a picture or a letter card. On a given signal play some game show music. The children must find the letters and picture that connect together to make a four-letter word. The first group to 'connect' each win a point for their team. Count the points up and give the winning team a medal each.

Focus of Learning

- To practise blending and segmenting CVCC and CCVC words for reading and spelling

Practical Activities

- Play 'Card Connect'. Deal each player in the group a card with a picture representing a four-letter word and four letter cards. Each player chooses a letter card to pass on and on a given signal they all pass their unwanted card to the right. The object of the game is to be the first player to spell the four-letter word that corresponds with their picture.

- Play 'Phoneme Fours'. Make an A3-sized blank connect four grid and place in the middle of the table. Give each child a set of counters; each player should have a different colour. Pick a picture card out of a bag or box. The picture cards should represent a range of words with three, four or five phonemes. The child must work out how many phonemes are in the word. If it has four phonemes they may put one of their counters on the grid. The object of the game is to be the first player to get four counters in a row.

- Play 'Four Letters Galore'. Collect a selection of objects that are spelled with four letters. Group the objects together on a tray or table. Give each child in the group a whiteboard and pen. Ask the children to look closely at the objects and on a given signal they must write as many of the four-letter words as they can on their whiteboard. A variation to this game could be to cover all the objects and make it a memory as well as a spelling game. You could also remove one of the objects and the children must try and work out which object is missing.

- Play 'Jigsaw Fours'. Prepare a selection of pictures representing four-letter words, cut into four jigsaw pieces and place them in a feely box. Give each child a four-letter word. They must take it in turns to pull a jigsaw piece out of the feely box. If it is one of the pieces of their four-letter word they may keep it, otherwise they must put it back. The first player to complete their jigsaw is the winner.

Display Ideas

- Create a large connect four game. Make giant counters with letters on them to make four-letter words. Some of the counters could have question marks so that the display becomes interactive; the children must work out the missing letters in the words.

- Paint large pictures of four-letter words and cut them into four jigsaw pieces. Arrange on board with letters on top.

Cross-curricular Links

- **MATHS** – Teach children how to play connect four and the strategies involved. Explain that this is problem-solving and look at a range of other problem-solving games.

- **DESIGN & TECHNOLOGY** – Use a range of construction kits and look at the different ways of connecting things. Look at ways of fixing and connecting models using recyclable materials, for example, glue, Sellotape, tying together etc. Extend this to looking at ways real objects have been connected.

- **PSHCE** – Play a range of cooperative, teamwork games that involve connections, for example, children hold hands and you tangle the children up. They need to untangle themselves without letting go of each others' hands.

Dinosaurumpus

Whole-class Starter

- Read the story *Bumpus Jumpus Dinosaurumpus* by Tony Mitton and Guy Parker-Rees (Orchard Books). Explain to the children that the book has a rhythm and that the author has created this by making the book rhyme. Ask the children if they know what a rhyming word is. Reread the book again and ask the children to listen carefully for the rhyming words. Discuss their answers. On the board make a list of words they notice that rhyme.

Focus of Learning

- To understand what rhyme is and recognise rhyming patterns

- Give each child a dinosaur-shaped laminated piece of paper. On the board place a large word. Ask the children to look at the word and write down on their dinosaurs as many rhyming words as they can think of. Discuss their answers.

- Make a set of cards that include words and pictures from different rhyming families. Give one card to each child and ask the children to move around the classroom or large space, quietly saying the word on their card. The children must listen to each others' words and find the other children that belong with them to create a rhyming family. Once they have found all of their rhyming family they must shout "Dinosaurumpus!" and do a dinosaur dance.

- Play 'Carpet Rumpus'. On the board place a three-letter phoneme word, for example, 'hat' or 'dog'. On seeing the word the children must call out a word that rhymes, for example, for 'dog' the children call out "fog", "log" etc. If more than one child calls out at the same time they have created a 'Carpet Rumpus' and they all say the rhyming chorus from the book.

Practical Activities

- Play 'T-Rex Rumpus'. Make a set of cards that include words from different rhyming families. For example, 'hat', 'cat', 'mat', 'bat' etc., or 'dog', 'log', 'hog', 'fog' etc. Put the words from each different rhyming family on a picture of a different dinosaur from the story. Place these word cards around the hall or large space. Choose one of the children to be the 'Terrible T-Rex' and give them a bib with a picture of a T-Rex on it. Split the group into five teams or pairs and give each team a rhyming family to collect. On a given signal one child from each team runs to collect a dinosaur and then returns to their team and then the next child does the same. Meanwhile the T-Rex tries to tag the children who are collecting the cards. If a player from a team is tagged they must put all of their cards back and start again. The first team to collect all of their cards is the winner.

- Play 'Running Rumpus'. Play this game in a hall or large space. Put up six large pictures with corresponding words around the edge of the hall. In a bag or box in the middle of the hall put an assortment of words that rhyme with the pictures around the hall. Play some music, the children dance around the hall and when the music stops they must choose a picture to run to. Pull a word out of the bag or box. If it rhymes with their chosen picture they are out of the game. Continue until you have a winner.

- Make a Bumpus Jumpus Dinosaurumpus rhyming book using the rhyming chorus from the story as a model for their own ideas.

Display Ideas

- Paint and collage a large dinosaur based on the front cover of the book. Add rhyming words.

- Paint and collage a variety of dinosaurs based on dinosaurs from the book. Mount children's own versions of Bumpus Jumpus Dinosaurumpus onto the dinosaurs.

- Paint and collage a large T-Rex. Surround it with rhyming words for children to put together into families.

- Colour mix shades of green and paint giant leaves to create a jungle effect.

Cross-curricular Links

- **ART** – Wet paper and drop red, orange and yellow inks onto it to create a sunset background. Use black paper to cut out and stick on a dancing dinosaur silhouette.

  Using felt and thread make a beanie dinosaur.

- **DESIGN & TECHNOLOGY** – Using recyclable materials ask the children to create their own dinosaur.

  Using chicken wire, newspaper and modroc ask the children to work as a group to create a dinosaur.

- **SCIENCE** – Investigate features of different dinosaurs and create a fact file.

Sally Syllable

Whole-class Starter

- Enter the classroom in role as 'Sally Syllable' carrying a selection of percussion instruments. Explain that Sally Syllable is really clever when it comes to spelling words. Tell the children that you can break words down into little chunks that make it easier for them when they are spelling. These chunks are called syllables. Out of a 'syllable sack' pull out an object that contains one syllable. Show the children how to say this word, for example, 'frog'. Explain that your mouth only moves once and this means it has one syllable. Show the children several more examples. Repeat this with words that contain two, three and four syllables.

- Play 'The Sound of Syllables'. Invite different children to go and collect an object from around the classroom area. Choose one of the objects. Ask the children to work with a talk partner and to discuss how many syllables they think make up that word. Ask the children to hold up the appropriate number of fingers to show how many syllables there are in that word. Choose one of the instruments and beat out the syllables so that the children can hear the syllables. Repeat several times ensuring that you include one, two, three and four syllable words.

- Play 'Slice the Syllables'. Give each pair a whiteboard and pen. Prepare on the interactive whiteboard or on large flashcards a selection of pictures and words that include a different number of syllables. Show the group a picture and the corresponding word. Ask the children to write the word on their whiteboard and then draw a slash to demarcate the syllables. Discuss their choices.

Focus of Learning

- To discriminate syllables in multi-syllabic words

Practical Activities

● Play 'Sort your Syllables'. Make a selection of syllable sacks that contain a picture of a word and the word broken down in to the appropriate syllables on cards. For example, 'dinosaur' would include a picture of a dinosaur and the word cards 'din', 'o', 'saur'. Give each small group a syllable sack and on a given signal they must take out their cards and put them into the correct order. Each group must then sound out their syllables to the rest of the group. A variation of this game is to have blank syllable cards on which the children must write the appropriate syllables to match the picture and then put into the correct order.

● Play 'Syllable Charades'. Give each child a picture card. The object of the game is to mime the word to the rest of the group using the amount of syllables it contains and by acting out either the whole word or the different syllables. For example, for 'lion' = 'li – on', the child would mime two syllables (hold up two fingers) and then they could roar or act out the first syllable by lying down.

● Play 'Secret Syllables'. Make a set of cards that include a picture on one side and the corresponding word broken down into syllables on the other. On each card remove one or two syllables and replace with a question mark. Give each child a whiteboard. Each child takes it in turn to pick out a card. They must read the card to find out which syllable is missing and use their phonic knowledge to help them write the word on their whiteboard. The children could then put the word in a sentence.

● Play 'Search for a Syllable'. Make a set of picture cards and place around the classroom or school. Ask the children to find a card and on a whiteboard try and write the appropriate word using the correct syllables.

Display Ideas

● Ask the children to paint and collage a selection of large percussion instruments.

● Paint and collage a Sally Syllable face.

● Ask the children to write the syllables for different words in large writing. Mount these on music notes.

● Ask the children to draw and colour a picture of their choice. Cut the pictures into the number of the syllables in that word. Mount the chopped up picture on paper and display the syllables underneath.

Cross-curricular Links

● **MUSIC** – Using a variety of percussion instruments, give the children a picture card and ask them to beat out the word using the correct number of syllables.

● **MATHS** – Play 'Syllable Sums'. Make a selection of small picture cards and place in a bag or box. Give each child a whiteboard and pen. The children take it in turns to pick out two picture cards. They must count the syllables on each card and work out the appropriate sum. For example, a child might pick out pictures of a dinosaur and a television. The sum they would write would be '3 + 4 = 7'.

A Royal Row

Whole-class Starter

- In role as the Royal Princess, explain that Mama, Queen of Vowels, and Papa, King of Consonants, keep arguing and fighting with each other. Mama thinks her vowels are the most important letters in the kingdom, but Papa disagrees and says his consonants are just as important because without them the vowels would be pointless. Show the children all the king's consonants and explain that they must be important because there are so many. Then show them the five vowels ('a', 'e', 'i', 'o', 'u') and say that they are very rare so they must also be important. Suggest that the most important letters must be the letters that can make the best words. Look at the king's consonants and with the children's help try to make a three-letter word. Then look at the queen's vowels and with the children's help try to make a three-letter word. Suggest mixing the vowels and consonants. Invite them to show you what happens when vowels are mixed with consonants.

- Play 'Under and Over'. Make some very large laminated words (three or four letters) depending on the children's ability. These words could also be prepared on an interactive whiteboard. Invite a child to underline the vowels in the word and draw an arc above the consonants. After several goes ask the children to work with a partner and give them each a whiteboard and a pen. Show the children a word and ask them to write the word on their board and underline the vowels in the word and draw an arc above the consonants. This activity can be extended to either showing the children a picture or saying the word orally.

- Play 'Vowel or Consonant'. Ask the children to stand in a circle. Place a selection of letters in a 'royal' box and put it in the middle of the circle. Play some music and ask the children to pass a 'royal crown' around. When the music stops, the child holding the crown must pick a letter from the royal box and identify if it is a vowel or a consonant.

Focus of Learning
- To understand vowels and consonants

Practical Activities

- Play 'Sieve the Sand'. Using plastic letters place them in a sandpit, ensuring that they are well hidden. Ask the children to take it in turns to sieve the sand and find a letter. They must tell the other children in the group what letter it is and whether it is a consonant or vowel. The letters are placed on the board until each child has had a turn. Once they have all had a go, together they look at their letters and identify how many vowels they have, how many consonants they have and what words they can make using the vowels and consonants.

- Play 'Roll and Mould'. Make a dice with the word 'vowel' on three sides and 'consonant' on the other three sides. Give each child in the group a large piece of Play-Doh or modelling clay. Each child takes it in turn to roll the dice. If it lands on 'vowel' they must attempt to make a vowel letter using the Play-Doh. If it lands on 'consonant' they must attempt to make a consonant letter.

- Play 'The Royal Roll'. Make a large chequered board and cover in an equal number of vowel and consonant letters. Split the group into two teams: the Queen of Vowels and the King of Consonants. Ask the children to sit around the chequered board. The children take it in turns to roll a small hoop (quoit) or ball onto the chequered board. The object of the game is to try and make the ball or hoop land on their appropriate letter. For example, if they are in the Queen of Vowels team they need to collect vowels. The first team to collect five letters wins the game. To add excitement to the game you could put several jester pictures on the board and if they land on a jester they must put all their letters back.

Display Ideas

- Paint and collage a large king, queen and princess.

- Make a consonant and vowel collage picture. Using newspapers and magazines ask the children to cut out a selection of consonants and vowels. Arrange the letters on a coloured background.

- Cut out a large vowel shape. Ask the children to design a vowel pattern on their shape using all five vowels.

- Ask the children to write giant three-, four- or five-letter words but miss out either a vowel or a consonant in each word.

They must replace the letter with a picture of a crown for the missing vowel or a gold coin for the missing consonant. This could form part of an interactive display so children could try and guess each others' words.

Cross-curricular Links

- **LITERACY** – Write a letter to the king or queen explaining that vowels and consonants are equally important and why we need them both.

- **MATHS** – Introduce the children to the royal coins that belong to the consonant king. Encourage the children to recognise 1p, 2p, 5p, 10p, 20p, 50p and £1 coins. Extend this further to addition and subtraction of money.

- **HISTORY** – Discuss with the children:
  What is a king or queen?
  How does someone become a king or queen?
  Where do they live? What do they wear? What is their job?

The Long and Short of It

Focus of Learning

- To differentiate between the long and short vowel phonemes

Whole-class Starter

- In role dressed as a train conductor, explain that there are two carriages – one is the long-vowel carriage and one is the short-vowel carriage – and it is your job to ensure that everybody gets on the correct carriage. Show the children examples of short vowels: 'a', 'e', 'i', 'o' and 'u', as in 'cat', 'leg', 'pig', 'dog' and 'bus'; then show them examples of long vowels: 'ai', 'ee', 'igh', 'oa' and 'oo', as in 'train', 'bee', 'night', 'boat' and 'moon'. Tell them that they need to know their long and short vowels so they can get on the correct carriage. Ask them to work with a partner and give each pair a long-vowel flag and a short-vowel flag. Say words and if they are long vowels the children wave the long-vowel flag. If they are short vowels they wave the short-vowel flag. Write the phoneme on the board.

- Play 'Walking Vowels'. Make a set of picture cards with pictures of short- and long-vowel words. For example, 'train', 'dog', 'moon', 'bus' etc. Give each child a card and ask them to identify their vowel phoneme and walk around the class saying their phoneme until they locate the other children who have the same phoneme. The object is to find all the children who have the same vowel phoneme. Ask the children to identify their phoneme and explain what type of vowel it is. Repeat several times.

- Play 'Voice your Vowels'. Make a set of laminated trains or flags with pictures containing short and long vowels on one side and the corresponding grapheme on the other side. Begin by showing the children the picture and asking them to identify if the word has a short or long vowel. The children respond by saying "Short" or "Long". Then progress to asking the children to call out the correct phoneme when shown a picture. Progress again to asking the children to collectively call out the correct phoneme when shown just the grapheme. See how fast the children call out the phonemes.

Practical Activities

- Play 'The Vowel Train'. Make a set of long train playing boards with each vowel on a carriage. Make a set of picture cards that correspond to the different vowel phonemes. The children take it in turns to pick a picture and cover the corresponding carriage. For example, if they pick a cat they cover the 'a' short vowel phoneme. The object is to cover all the vowel phonemes on your train.

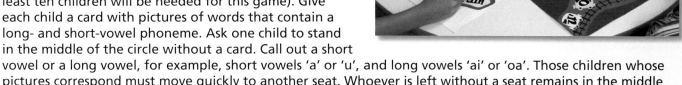

- Play 'All Aboard'. Sit the children in a circle on chairs (at least ten children will be needed for this game). Give each child a card with pictures of words that contain a long- and short-vowel phoneme. Ask one child to stand in the middle of the circle without a card. Call out a short vowel or a long vowel, for example, short vowels 'a' or 'u', and long vowels 'ai' or 'oa'. Those children whose pictures correspond must move quickly to another seat. Whoever is left without a seat remains in the middle of the circle. After each instruction the children swap cards with the child on their left. If you say "all aboard", everybody has to move and find a new seat!

- Play 'The Long and Short of it!' Make a set of bingo-style boards with pictures of long- and short-vowel words in each square. Ensure that there is enough space to write the corresponding word. Make two dice: one with the long-vowel phonemes on and one with the short-vowel phonemes. On the extra dice sides place a picture of a train or a flag. The children take it in turn to roll the dice and whichever vowel phoneme it lands on they must write the word by the corresponding picture on their board. If they roll a train or flag picture they must miss a go! The object is to write all the corresponding words on their boards.

Display Ideas

- Use recyclable material to make a 3D train for display.

- Draw, paint and collage large pictures that correspond to the vowel phonemes.

- Collect objects that correspond to vowel phonemes that can be used for an interactive table-top display.

- Ask the children to choose a vowel phoneme and to paint it using one bold colour. The children can either draw or cut out collage pictures that correspond to that phoneme and stick them on or around their vowel phoneme. For example, 'ai = train, rain, chain, drain' etc.

Cross-curricular Links

- **LITERACY** – Give each child a train shape zigzag book and on each carriage section they must write a long- or short-vowel phoneme and either draw pictures or write words that relate to that vowel phoneme. The title of the booklet could be 'The Vowel Express'.

- **ART** – Ask the children to choose a long or short vowel and draw a picture that includes as many of that particular phoneme as possible.

- **DESIGN & TECHNOLOGY** – Use a variety of construction kits to construct a variety of different style trains.

The Snail and the Whale

Whole-class Starter

Focus of Learning

- To use common spelling patterns, 'ay', 'ai' and 'a-e'

- Read the story *The Snail and the Whale* by Julia Donaldson and Axel Scheffler (Macmillian Children's Books). Ask them to identify what the differences are between the snail and the whale. After you have discussed the different features and characteristics of the animals, ask the children what differences and similarities they notice about the words 'snail' and 'whale'. Discuss with the children the long-vowel phonemes 'ai' and 'a-e'. Explain that they sound the same but are spelled differently. Using the words 'snail' and 'whale', show the children the phonemes 'ai' and 'a-e'. Ask the children if they can identify any more words that have the phonemes 'ai' and 'a-e'. Make a list on the board.

- Play 'Mix and Match'. Make a set of laminated picture cards of words that contain the 'ai', 'a-e' and 'ay' phonemes. Make a set of corresponding cards that have just the phonemes 'ai', 'a-e' and 'ay' written on them. Give each child a card. Play some appropriate music and ask the children to find a partner who has a picture card or a phoneme card that corresponds with their own. Repeat several times.

- Play 'What Does it Say?' Make a set of large cards that have anagrams of different 'ai', 'a-e' or 'ay' words. This could also be prepared on an interactive whiteboard. Give each child a whiteboard and pen. Reveal an anagram and ask the children to unscramble the word and write the correct spelling on their board. Discuss the strategies that will aid the children in working the words out. For example, 'ay' is usually at the end of a word and 'ai' is usually in the middle of a word.

Practical Activities

- Play 'Hoorah! I Spy an "ai", "a-e" or "ay" '. Give each child in the group a copy of the book *The Snail and the Whale*. Also give them an A3-sized sheet of paper with a picture of a whale, snail and the bay on. The children will also need a pencil and a magnifying glass. Ask the children to look through the book and identify different 'ai', 'a-e' or 'ay' words. If they find a word they must write it in the correct place on their piece of paper. For example, the word 'away' would be written in the picture of the bay.

- Play 'Snail Trail'. Make a trail around the school grounds for the children to follow using silver thread. Along the trail place laminated pictures of the snail from the story. On the back of each snail write an 'ai', 'a-e' or 'ay' anagram word. The children must follow the trail and unscramble the words as they find them and write them on a whiteboard.

- Play 'Save the Whale'. Make each child in the group a laminated playing board in the shape of a whale with ten 'ai', 'a-e' or 'ay' phonemes all over the whale picture. Make a set of water droplet cards with pictures of 'ay', 'ai' and 'a-e' words on them and place them in a bag. The children should take it in turns to pull a card out of the bag. If they can match the picture to the correct grapheme on their playing board they may cover their grapheme with a droplet. If they can't they must put the droplet back in the bag or box. The first child to cover all their graphemes saves the whale and wins the game.

Display Ideas

- Paint and collage a large snail and whale for display.

- Using collage materials create a bay scene.

- Ask the children to write large words that include the 'ai', 'a-e' and 'ay' phonemes.

- Ask the children to create their own setting that could be visited by the whale and the snail. The children could draw and use pencil crayons to create colour. Challenge them to include a variety of 'ai', 'a-e', or 'ay' pictures.

Cross-curricular Links

- **PSHCE** – Read a selection of whale books that highlight the issue of whales in danger. For example, *Dear Greenpeace* by Simon James (Walker Books Ltd) or *The Whales' Song* by Dyan Sheldon and Gary Blythe (Red Fox). Ask the children to write a letter or design a 'save the whale' poster.

  Extend this topic to look at other endangered animals. Organise a whole school 'Concerned about conservation' week. Discuss issues such as pollution, endangered animals and preserving habitats and create a display as shown.

Tea with Bernard the Bee

Whole-class Starter

- At the start of the lesson show the children an invitation that has arrived from Bernard the Bee inviting the children to tea at his beehive:

Dear Children,

I'm writing this invite to see if you're free,

To come to my beehive for tea with me.

Tea will be served at half-past three,

With peaches and cream in the big oak tree,

If you can come it will fill me with glee,

Please come and have tea with Bernard the Bee!

Love Bernard x x x

Focus of Learning

- To use common spelling patterns 'ee', 'ea' and 'e-e'

- Read the invitation with the children and discuss the words that rhyme. Identify that the reason that these words rhyme is because they have the same phoneme at the end. Ask the children which phoneme they have in common and identify that it is the long vowels 'ee', 'ea' or 'e' that sound the same. Invite children to come out and circle words that contain 'ee', 'ea' or 'e'. Explain that though these are all different graphemes, they all sound the same.

- Play 'What can you see? Is it an "ee"?' Use an interactive whiteboard (or make a giant picture) to create a scene that contains lots of pictures of things with the 'ee', 'ea' or 'e' phoneme mixed in with other pictures of things that do not contain this phoneme. Give the children a minute to look at the scene and then hide the picture and the children must record as many things they can remember from the scene that have the 'ee', 'ea' or 'e' phoneme on a whiteboard. Discuss the children's responses.

- Play 'Cross the Sea to the Correct "ee" or "ea" '. Use a large piece of blue fabric to create a 'sea' dividing the area in two. On one side place a large laminated 'ee' grapheme and on the other side a large laminated 'ea' grapheme. Ask the children to stand on the sea and then call out a word containing 'ee' or 'ea'. The children decide which grapheme is in that word and move to that side. For example, if you call out the word 'cheese' the correct place to stand is the 'ee' side.

Practical Activities

- Play 'Tea with Bernard the Bee'. Set up a tea party outside under a tree using teacups, saucers, teapot etc. Make a set of laminated pictures that will fit into the bottom of the teacup. Each child will need a whiteboard and pen. Each child in the group sits by their teacup and on a given signal they look into it and discover what picture Bernard has poured for them. The children attempt to write the correct word on their whiteboard. If they are correct they get to have a piece of Bernard's imaginary cake!

- Give the children a honeycomb-shaped piece of paper (A3 size). Ask the children to pick either 'ee' or 'ea' and fill their honeycomb with pictures and words that contain that grapheme.

- Play 'Buzzz off Bernard the Bee'. Make a set of laminated bee pictures with pictures of things that contain 'ee' or 'ea' on them. Place them around a room or large open space. Give each child in the group a fly swatter. On a given signal hold up either an 'ee' or 'ea'. The children must buzzz to a corresponding picture and swat it! An extension to this activity would be to ask the children to put their word into a sentence or write it down on a whiteboard.

Display Ideas

- Paint and collage a giant Bernard the Bee and display him with an 'ee' on one wing and an 'ea' on the other. Include the invitation on the display.

- Using polystyrene tiles ask the children to design a bee printing tile and print using printing ink and a roller. Add bee colours using oil pastels.

- Design a large teapot and teacups.

- Using chalk pastels ask the children to draw and pastel pictures of 'ee' and 'ea' words. Mount onto droplet shapes.

Cross-curricular Links

- **ART** – Make a clay teapot and cup and saucer set. Paint the finished cup and saucer using poster paint. Varnish to create a shiny effect.

- **SCIENCE** – Learn facts about bees and pollination.

- **ICT** – Plan a route to get Bernard back to the beehive using a programmable toy.

- **ASSEMBLY** – Create a board in the school hall that promotes the idea of children making suggestions to improve the school. Call the board 'Be as Busy as a Bee'. The children write suggestions on laminated bees. On the board put a large bee with a speech bubble saying 'Be a busy bee and write a suggestion on me!' Discuss the suggestions in a weekly assembly.

I Spy with my Little Eye

Whole-class Starter

- In role dressed as an optician, tell the children you have come to check their eyes. On the interactive whiteboard prepare large pictures of objects that contain 'igh', 'ie' and 'i-e', for example, 'light', 'pie' and 'smile'. Hide part of the picture and reveal a bit at a time. Ask the children to discuss what they think it is. Once they have decided, ask children to reveal the picture. Repeat several times. Show the children all the pictures and ask them to say the words. Discuss what they all have in common. Explain that they all contain the long vowel 'i'.

- Reveal to the children the spellings of each of the pictures you used in the earlier activity. Highlight the long vowel in each of the words and ask the children what they notice. For example, there are different ways to spell the same long-vowel phoneme 'i'. Play 'I Spy' with the children. Sit the children in a circle and place a selection of objects or pictures in the middle of the circle. Say "I spy with my little eye an object that contains the long-vowel phoneme 'igh' ". The children look at the objects and decide which object they think contains this long-vowel phoneme. If they guess correctly remove the object.

- Play 'I Spy My "i" '. Make a set of picture cards that contain the long-vowel phoneme 'i' and a set of corresponding cards that have the long-vowel graphemes 'igh', 'ie' or 'i-e' on them. Give one half of the class a picture card each and the other half grapheme cards. Play some appropriate music and ask the children to walk around slowly showing each other their cards. On a given signal the children must try and find a partner. For example, a child holding a picture of a light would try and find a child holding a grapheme card 'igh'.

Focus of Learning

- To use the common spelling patterns 'igh', 'ie' and 'i-e'

Practical Activities

- Make a set of 'Eye Spy' books with cut-out eyes on alternate pages. Behind each eye the children must draw pictures of objects that contain the long-vowel phonemes 'igh', 'ie' and 'i-e'. Underneath the pictures they must write the correct graphemes or a sentence that contains that word.

- Collect a set of objects that contain the long-vowel phonemes 'igh', 'ie' or 'i-e' and place them in the middle of the table. Give each child a whiteboard and a pen. Let the children look at all the objects on the table and then cover the objects. The children must write down as many objects as they can remember that have the long-vowel phonemes 'igh', 'ie' or 'i-e'. An extension to this would be to just remove one object, add another object or include objects that don't contain the correct long-vowel phoneme.

- Play 'Spy the "igh", "ie" and "i-e"'. Make pictures of words containing the phonemes 'igh', 'ie' and 'i-e', mounted on eye-shaped paper. Place them around the school or outside area. Make a selection of 'igh', 'ie' and 'i-e' graphemes on cards. In pairs the children take a grapheme card from a box or bag and race to find a picture that contains their phoneme. If they are correct they get another card and the chance to find another picture. If they are incorrect they must put the picture back and try to find the correct one. The object of the game is to collect as many pictures as possible.

- Play 'Splat the Right "i"'. Using the interactive whiteboard make a multimedia presentation that involves the phonemes 'igh', 'ie' and 'i-e' flashing on the board. Make a set of picture cards of words containing these long-vowel phonemes. Split the children into two teams. A child from each team stands with their back to the board and a splatter in their hand. Reveal a picture; the children turn and race to splat the correct 'igh', 'ie' or 'i-e' when it flashes on the board.

Display Ideas

- Make large 3D eyes using card and paper. Use as a border around the display.

- Ask the children to draw large pictures of words that include the phonemes 'igh', 'ie' or 'i-e'. Use chalk or oil pastels. Ask the children to write the words that correspond with their picture in large bold writing, but miss out the 'igh', 'ie' or 'i-e' and replace it with a picture of a giant eye.

- Ask the children to bring an object in from home that contains the phonemes 'igh', 'ie' or 'i-e'. The children take a photo of part of their object and use on the display with the quote 'I Spy with my Little Eye'.

Cross-curricular Links

- **LITERACY** – Make a board that contains lots of 'igh', 'ie' and 'i-e' pictures. Ask the children to select five pictures from the board and write a creative story.

- **SCIENCE** – Ask the children to draw and label a picture of the human eye. Investigate facts about the eye. Discuss with the children different parts of the eye.

- **PSHCE** – Invite an optician to discuss eyes with the children and why it is important to protect and keep them safe.

Joseph and His Rainbow Coat

Whole-class Starter

- In role dressed as 'Joseph' in a rainbow-coloured coat, retell the story in your own words. Explain that Joseph's dad gave him the coat. Tell the children it is a rainbow coat and his name is Joseph and all of these words have got a long 'o' phoneme. On the board write Joseph's name, the word 'rainbow' and the word 'coat' with the phonemes 'ow', 'oa' and 'o-e' highlighted. Explain that although they sound the same they are all spelled differently.

- Play 'Roll a Rainbow'. Make a large black and white coat and place on the board. Make laminated strips in the different colours of the rainbow. On each strip put a picture that contains the long-vowel phoneme 'o' and the corresponding spelling but with the 'o' grapheme missing. Give each child a laminated strip. Make a dice that has two sides with the 'ow' grapheme, two with the 'oa' grapheme and two with the 'o-e' grapheme. Roll the dice and if a child has a word with that grapheme missing they write it on their strip and place it on the coat on the board. The object is to make Joseph a new rainbow coat.

- Play 'I Spy an "o" Joe!' Collect an array of objects that contain the long-vowel 'o' phoneme, for example, 'boat', 'bow tie', 'coat', 'float', 'soap', 'rainbow', 'crow', 'note' and 'rope'. Ask the children to sit in a circle in pairs and give them a laminated coat and a pen. Place the objects in the middle of the circle. Play *Go, Go, Go Joseph* from the musical *Joseph and the Amazing Technicolor Dreamcoat* (Original Cast Recording and Andrew Lloyd Webber). Allow the children to look at the objects whilst the music is playing. When the music stops cover the objects with Joseph's rainbow coat. Ask the children to write down as many things as they can remember. Award a point for each word that is spelled correctly.

Focus of Learning

- To use the common spelling patterns 'ow', 'oa' and 'o-e'

Practical Activities

- Play 'Joseph's Rainbow Coat'. Make a set of laminated playing boards with plain coats on them. Make a second set of cards in the seven colours of the rainbow with pictures of words containing the 'ow', 'oa' and 'o-e' phonemes in them. The children take it in turns to pick a colour card and if they can identify which of the phonemes the word contains they add it to their plain coat. The object of the game is to fill their coat with the seven colours of the rainbow.

- Give each child in the group a coat-shaped piece of paper. Ask the children to use coloured pencils and pens and fill their coat with as many 'ow', 'oa' and 'o-e' words as they can.

- Play 'Go, Go, Go Joseph'. Attach sets of laminated rainbow-coloured strips with pictures of 'ow', 'oa' and 'o-e' words to tag rugby belts or Velcro-style belts. Chose two or three children to wear the belts. Split the remainder of the children into teams of two or three. A player from each team takes it in turns to chase the children wearing the belts (allocate a suitable area in which to play the game). They must attempt to grab a coloured strip and having done so return to their team members and together write the correct 'ow', 'oa', or 'o-e' word. The team that collects all seven colours of the rainbow and correctly writes the words is the winner.

Display Ideas

- Paint and collage a large picture of Joseph in his multicoloured coat.

- Chalk pastel pictures containing the phonemes 'ow', 'oa', and 'o-e'.

- Make a rainbow coat with lift-up-flap action. On the top of each colour ask the children to draw and pen a picture of an 'ow', 'oa', or 'o-e' word. Underneath the colour ask the children to write the correct word.

- Challenge the children to choose a colour from the rainbow and ask them to colour mix as many different shades of that colour as they can. Use the strips to create a giant rainbow.

- Use binca and thread to sew a multicoloured rainbow.

Cross-curricular Links

- **R.E.** – Retell the story of Joseph. Encourage the children to re-enact the story through role play. Discuss the different sections of the story and how Joseph felt at the beginning, middle and end of the story. Discuss the actions of his brothers.

- **LITERACY** – Ask the children to create a cartoon strip that tells the story of Joseph. Encourage the children to use speech bubbles and think bubbles.

I Love You, Blue Kangaroo

Whole-class Starter

- Read the story *I Love You, Blue Kangaroo* by Emma Chichester Clark (Andersen Press Ltd). Discuss the title with the children and ask them what long-vowel phoneme they can hear. Identify the phonemes and write them on the board. Discuss with the children that although they sound the same they are spelled differently. Explain to the children when to use all the long-vowel phonemes 'oo', 'ue', 'ew' and 'u-e'. Make some big laminated cards with the graphemes on and place on the board.

- Play 'Choose Your "oo"'. Using the grapheme cards from the last activity, place them around a large space or hall. With the children standing in the middle of the area, play some appropriate music such as *I Want to be Like You* from *The Jungle Book Soundtrack* (Walt Disney Records). The children move around the area and when the music stops they choose a grapheme to stand by. Call out an 'oo' word, or pick one out of a bag. For example, 'spoon', 'glue', 'blew' or 'flute'. The children who are standing by that grapheme are out of the game. The game continues until one child is remaining.

- Play 'What's the "oo" Blue Kangaroo?' Make a set of laminated kangaroo paddles that have an 'oo' long-vowel phoneme on each one (use the graphemes 'oo', 'ew', 'eu' and 'u-e'). Ask the children to work with a partner and give each pair a set of paddles to share. Say a word or show a picture of a word that has one of the graphemes in it. The children discuss which grapheme they think is in the word and they hold up the correct kangaroo paddle. You could then write the word on the board.

Focus of Learning

- To learn the long-vowel phonemes 'oo', 'ue', 'ew' and 'u-e'

Practical Activities

- Play 'Kangaroo Bounce'. Make a set of picture cards with the different 'oo' alternatives; 'oo', 'ue', 'ew', 'u-e'. Place the cards around a large space. Split the group into two or three teams and give each team a space hopper. Place a whiteboard and pen by each grapheme 'oo' card. The first child from each team sits on their space hopper. Call out a word and the children must bounce to the correct grapheme card and write the word on a whiteboard. The fastest child wins a point for their team and at the end of the session the team with the most points wins.

- Play 'I Spy an "oo" Do You?' Make a set of kangaroo-shaped booklets, with a page for each 'oo' grapheme. Give each child a magnifying glass and a selection of books. Ask the children to find as many graphemes as they can from the books and write them on the correct page in their kangaroo booklet. For example, if they found the word 'glue' they would write it on the 'ue' page. Discuss with the group the most common graphemes and the positions in the words. Ask if they notice any regularities or irregularities.

- Play 'Lose Your "oo"s'. Make a set of small 'oo' cards including all the different 'oo' graphemes. Make a set of picture cards that correspond with the grapheme cards and place them in a bag or box. Give each child a bumbag or an item that could represent a kangaroo's pouch. The children place six grapheme cards each in their pouch. They each pick a picture card out of the bag or box and if it corresponds to one of their grapheme cards they can remove it. For example, a child may pick out a picture of a flute and if they have the 'u-e' grapheme card they can remove it from their pouch. The object of the game is to lose all their 'oos'.

Display Ideas

- Paint and collage a giant picture of Lily and the Blue Kangaroo.

- Chalk pastel pictures of the different toy animals in the story holding a picture of a word with the 'oo', 'ew', 'ue' or 'u-e' phoneme.

- Use powder paint to colour mix leaves in shades of green. Use to create a garden effect border. Paint giant flowers to add to the garden.

- Chalk a pastel picture of Blue Kangaroo. Look at ideas from the book to inspire children to pastel him in a variety of different poses.

Cross-curricular Links

- **PSHCE** – Discuss feelings of loneliness and being left out. Discuss with the children if they have ever felt left out or left somebody out of a game. How did they feel? Ask how can we make people not feel left out.

- **DESIGN & TECHNOLOGY** – Invite the children to bring their favourite toy into class and ask them to design and make a bed to fit their toy.

- **HISTORY** – Discuss the characters in the story; they are all family members.

  Ask the children to talk about different family members they have. Invite them to draw a family tree or portrait.

Ed the Archaeologist

Whole-class Starter

- In role as Ed the Archaeologist, tell the children a story of how you discovered an Egyptian tomb. Show the children words that relate to your adventure, such as 'discovered', 'explored', 'uncovered', 'opened', 'revealed', 'astounded', 'surprised' and 'searched'. Explain there are words that exist in the present tense and words that exist in the past tense. Ask the children to look closely at the words. Do they notice anything? Explain that the words all end in 'ed' and this is how we can discover that words are from the past. Ask the children to circle the 'ed' on each word.

- Reveal a treasure chest and explain to the children that in the chest there are a mixture of words; some from the past and some from the present. Invite the children to sort the words into two hoops labelled 'past' and 'present'. For example, if they pull out 'looked' it would go in the 'past' hoop but if they pull out 'discover' it would go in the 'present' hoop.

- Play 'Pyramid Puzzle'. Make a set of large pyramids with words from the present tense on them. Hide the pyramids around the classroom. Invite one of the children to wear Ed's hat and go and discover a hidden pyramid. Ask the children to help you change the word from the present tense to the past tense. Include on the pyramids words that already end in 'e', and as these words are discovered discuss the rule 'if it ends in an "e" just add a "d" '. Also include words that require doubling the consonant.

Focus of Learning

- To learn about words with 'ed' (past tense)

Practical Activities

- Play 'Pyramids From the Past'. Make a set of laminated pyramids with anagrams of words written on them. The children must work out the word from the anagram and write it down on a card.

- Play 'Ed's Expedition'. Make a board game depicting Ed's expedition in the Egyptian desert. The board should include footsteps that the players move along. If the footstep they land on has a pyramid symbol they pick a pyramid card from the middle. On the pyramid cards are either present-tense words that they must change into past tense on a whiteboard, or instructions, for example, 'Discovered an empty tomb, miss a go'. The object of the game is to collect as many past-tense words as possible.

- Play 'Archaeologist Adventure'. Give the children a story beginning, for example, 'My name is Ed the Archaeologist and I discovered the secret of the Valley of the Kings. It all began when I …' Pull a present-tense word out of a bag that the children must change into the past tense and include in the next sentence of their story. Read and discuss the completed story.

Display Ideas

- Ask children to paint or pastel large bricks.

- Paint and collage a large Ed the Archaeologist.

- Ask children to write sentences that include 'ed' words and phrases and stick onto pyramids. Arrange pyramids with Ed's face poking out from behind with speech bubbles about the past-tense rules.

- Ask the children to design and paint death masks that Ed finds in his tomb.

Cross-curricular Links

- **MATHS** – Make a set of pyramid puzzles for the children to solve.

  Investigate 3D shapes and different kinds of pyramids.

- **HISTORY** – Learn about the Egyptian pyramids. Present information in a pyramid-shaped zigzag book.

- **LITERACY** – Ask children to make a pyramid-shaped wordsearch including 'ed' words.

Sing for Spring

Whole-class Starter

- In role as 'King of Spring' tell the children you love this time of year because everything related to spring links to his name. From a toy wheelbarrow pull out different pictures or objects relating to spring, for example, 'daffodil', 'frog', 'baby chick', 'lamb', 'tadpole', 'blossom' etc. Ask the children what they are. Elaborate on the words, for example, "They are not just daffodils, they are dancing daffodils" or "They are not just frogs, they are leaping frogs." Ask the children if they can identify the link ('ing'). Show the children some more objects or pictures and ask if they can make them link to the king's name.

Focus of Learning

- To investigate and learn spellings of words with 'ing' (present tense)

- Explain that the 'ing' in your name is useful for making lots of words. Challenge the children to 'sing the "ing" word'. Using the interactive whiteboard make movable text boxes with the parts of 'ing' words in each box. For example, 'ing' and 'a', 's', 't', 'r', 'w', 'th' and 'p'. The children can drag the boxes to make different words such as 'ring', 'string', 'thing' etc. Each time they make an 'ing' word they must sing the word. This can also be done using a standard whiteboard and large cards.

- Play 'Standing in an "ing" Ring'. This game should be played in a large space. Place hoops around the area. Make a set of 'ing' cards and other phoneme cards that, put together with 'ing', will make new words. Give each child a card and on a given signal the children must move around without talking and show each other their cards until they find one or more person(s) with whom they can make a word. For example, they might make a simple word like 'k-ing' or a more complex word like 's-t-r-ing'. Once they have made a word they should go and stand in a ring and shout "We've put our 'ing' in a ring!"

Practical Activities

- Play 'Ring the ing'. Make a giant wordsearch including a variety of 'ing' words. Make a six-sided dice. On three sides have a ring with 'ing' on, on two sides a 'thumbs down' symbol, and on the last side a 'thumbs up' symbol. Each child should have a different coloured bib or badge. If the dice lands on a ring they can circle an 'ing' word in their colour. If the dice lands on a thumbs down they can rub out one of their opponent's 'ing' words and if the dice lands on a 'thumbs up' they have 20 seconds to circle as many 'ing' words as possible.

- Play 'Ing with the King in Spring'. Make each child an A3-sized laminated board with a picture of the king and some smaller pictures related to springtime. Make laminated crowns with verbs on that relate to the springtime pictures, for example, 'leap', 'dance', 'fall', 'sway', 'swim', 'hop' etc. The children take it in turns to pull a word-card out of a bag. They must work out which springtime picture it is associated with and turn it into an 'ing' word, writing it underneath the correct picture. For example, if they pick out 'hop' they write underneath the frog, lamb or rabbit the word 'hopping'. The object of the game is to be the first to write underneath each of their pictures. The winner gets to wear the king's crown. An extension to this game would be to focus on applying the correct spelling rules to each word.

- Play 'Sing with the King'. Work in a small group with a selection of musical percussion instruments. Make a selection of 'ing' words on large laminated cards. Give each pair an 'ing' word that they must segment into different phonemes and choose a musical instrument to represent each phoneme. Invite the children to 'sing with the king' then perform their word to the group.

Display Ideas

- Draw, paint and collage pictures related to springtime.

- Ask children to write sentences associated with spring and including 'ing' words.

- Paint and collage giant kites and add 'ing' words onto the kites.

- Collage a giant king and surround him with 'ing' words and musical notes.

- Interactive display – place a selection of musical instruments on display and challenge the children to take an 'ing' word and sing with the king.

Cross-curricular Links

- **LITERACY** – Write a spring poem based on *Why Does it Happen in Spring?* from *Harlequin: 44 Songs Round the Year* (A & C Black Publishers Ltd).

- **SCIENCE** – Go on a spring walk around the school grounds and identify signs of spring. Collect signs of spring on a journey stick or take photos.

- **DESIGN & TECHNOLOGY** – Make a jelly pond. Ask the children to describe the pond using 'ing' words.

Rigorous Roots – Root Words

Whole-class Starter

- In role as a gardener explain that you have bought these marvellous seeds but you are not sure what they will grow into because the packets have the names of the roots but don't have the names of the flowers they will grow into. Show the children the different packets and reveal the root names, for example, 'happy', 'care', 'cook' etc. Ask the children if they have got any suggestions what the root word might grow into. Write their suggestions on the board. Explain that they help with spelling because once they know how to spell the root it helps spell lots of other words.

Focus of Learning

- To collect and generate new words from root words

- Explain that some words have a root and from these roots different flowers can grow. Put a large flower complete with roots on the board (this could be made and stuck on or drawn). Add a root word onto the root and ask the children to work with a talk partner to think of different words that can grow from it. Explain that for the root to grow it needs a little bit of prefix and some suffix to make a new word. Write their suggestions on the petals of the flower.

- Play 'Flower Power'. Make a set of large laminated flower heads, big enough for a pair of children to write on. Write a root word on the board. Within a given time each pair of children must write as many words that they can think of that correspond to the root word.

Practical Activities

- Play 'The Route to Roots'. Make a set of laminated root words and a set of corresponding laminated prefixes and suffixes. Place the root words in a large plant pot and the prefixes and suffixes on the wall at the opposite end of the room. Split the group into two teams and give each a toy wheelbarrow. The first person in each team picks a root word out of the plant pot, puts it into their wheelbarrow and runs with it to the prefixes and suffixes. The child must match the root and then race back and hand the wheelbarrow over to the next child. The object of the game is to match correctly as many root words to the word endings.

- Give each child a flower-shaped booklet. Ask the children to write a root word on the pot and corresponding word endings on the petals.

- Play 'Greenfingers'. Make a set of laminated boards with a picture of a root, stem and flower centre on them. On the root area of each board write a different root word. Make a set of petal shapes with corresponding prefixes and suffixes on them. Each flower will need five or six petals. Also make a set of cards with 'weed killer' written on them. The children take it in turns to pick a petal out of a flower pot. If it corresponds to their root word they place it on their board and if it doesn't they put it back in the pot. If they pick a weed killer card they must put all their petals back and start again. The winner is the child who completes their flower first.

Display Ideas

- Paint and collage a gardener with a watering can.

- Paint and collage several large flowers.

- Design and make a large seed packet. Use the idea of the root word as the name of the plant and ask the children to illustrate the packet with a picture of what it might grow into.

- Make captions that include missing roots or missing endings.

- Make a giant plant and label the different parts for a science display.

Cross-curricular Links

- **DESIGN & TECHNOLOGY** – Design and make a flower mobile. Use a variety of card, paper and string. The children could add their own root word and corresponding suffixes and prefixes on the roots and petals.

- **ART** – Use a selection of felt, hessian and threads to create a flower design. Encourage the children to use a variety of stitching and colours.
  Use a view finder to look closely at different parts of a plant and reproduce the design on calico using a batik technique and fabric paint.

- **SCIENCE** – Learn about the different parts and the functions of a plant.
  Investigate the conditions for growing a plant.

Rumble in the Jungle

Whole-class Starter

Focus of Learning

- To learn the 'le' grapheme as an alternative spelling for the phoneme 'l'

- Read the book *Rumble in the Jungle* by Giles Andreae and David Wojtowycz (Orchard Books). Ask the children what they notice about the book. Discuss rhyme, rhythm, favourite animals etc. Ask the children to look carefully at the title and discuss what they notice. Circle the 'le' graphemes on the board and explain that 'rumble' and 'jungle' have the same ending. Explain that 'le' is an alternative way of spelling the phoneme 'l'. Ask the children to practise saying the phoneme 'l' by whispering it, shouting it etc.

- Show the children a variety of pictures of words that have the 'le' phoneme, for example, 'apple', 'castle', 'table', 'smile' etc. Encourage the children to say the phoneme. Discuss the fact that you cannot hear the 'e'.

- Play 'Jumble in the Jungle'. Prepare a jungle scene on the interactive whiteboard. Give each child a whiteboard and pen. Hide a variety of pictures amongst the jungle scene. As the pictures appear the children must decide if the picture has the 'le' phoneme in it and write the 'le' word on their whiteboards. Discuss the words they have collected.

Practical Activities

- Play 'I Spy a Rumble'. Prepare a large jungle scene with pictures of 'le' words hidden in the jungle. Give the children one minute to remember as many 'le' words as possible. Then cover up the picture and ask them to write down as many 'le' words as they can remember.

- Play 'Rumble in the Jungle'. Use an outside area for this game (preferably a nature area that might look like a jungle). Prepare lots of large jungle animal laminated pictures. Some of the pictures should be of 'le' words and some of non-'le' words. Hide the pictures. Ask the children to stand together in a hoop and on the sound of a hooter they must run and find an animal and return to the hoop. If their animal has a picture of an 'le' word on it and they can spell it correctly they can stay in the game, otherwise they are out. The winner is the last person to remain in the jungle. A variation of this game would be to have jumbled up 'le' words on the reverse and to challenge the children to unscramble them.

- Play 'Jungle Jigsaws'. Make a selection of jungle animal jigsaws. Place the jigsaws in the middle of the table. Make a selection of cards that have pictures of 'le'-ending words and some without 'le' endings. The children take it in turns to pick a card from a bag or box. If they pick a card that has an 'le' ending they must spell the word correctly and then take a piece of their jigsaw. The first person to complete a jigsaw wins the game.

Display Ideas

- Paint and collage animals from the jungle.

- Colour mix shades of green leaves to create a jungle scene.

- Ask the children to draw large pictures of 'le' words and hide them amongst the jungle scene.

- Ask the children to write 'le' words with the 'le' part of the word missing. Place on the jungle leaves.

Cross-curricular Links

- **LITERACY** – Play 'Word Detectives'. Give the children a selection of books and a magnifying glass. Ask them to find words containing the 'le' grapheme. The children write the words on a jungle leaf.

- **GEOGRAPHY** – Discuss with the children the types of animals that live in jungles and where they would find jungles.

- **DESIGN & TECHNOLOGY** – Make an animated animal jungle scene. Ask the children to paint pictures of a variety of jungle animals. Ask the children to design ways in which the animal can move so that when it moves it reveals a 'le' word. For example, the trunk of an elephant could lift up and underneath there would be a word.

Commotion in the Ocean

Whole-class Starter

- Read the book *The Commotion in the Ocean* by Giles Andreae and David Wojtowycz (Orchard Picturebooks). Ask the children to close their eyes and listen to you as you whisper the title "Commotion in the Ocean". Tell the children that there is a secret in the title and once they have guessed it they may open their eyes. After all the children have opened their eyes ask one child to reveal the secret. Explain to the class that the secret in the title is that both words have the same phoneme.

- Make a set of large cards with pictures of words containing the phonemes 'tion', 'cean' or 'sion' on one side and the word on the other. For example, 'station', 'ocean', 'lotion', 'action' and 'confusion'. Hold up the picture cards one at a time and ask the children to say the word but whisper the phonemes 'tion', 'cean' and 'sion'. Ask the children to look at your mouth when you say the phoneme and ask them to do it back to you. Turn over the flashcards and ask the children what they notice about the graphemes. Explain to them that there are three different ways to spell the phoneme. Turn the cards back over to reveal the pictures. Ask the children to sort the pictures according to the grapheme they contain.

Focus of Learning

- To recognise and spell the suffixes 'tion' and 'sion'

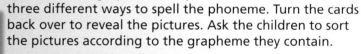

- Play 'Calm the Ocean'. You will need a large space. Make a set of large cards that contain a 'tion', 'cean' or 'sion' word. Give each child a card. Play the *Jaws* theme tune from *Jaws: Original Soundtrack* (John Williams) and ask the children to move around the hall silently like sharks. They must find all the other children whose words contain the same grapheme as theirs. When the children have sorted themselves into groups they must stand silently whilst you check their graphemes and confirm that the sea is now calm! This activity could be extended by giving the children picture cards and asking them to sort themselves into groups containing the same grapheme.

Practical Activities

- Play 'Catch of the Day'. Make a set of laminated sea creatures with pictures of 'tion', 'cean' or 'sion' words on them. Using a large children's paddling pool, split the children into three teams and give each team a fishing net and a bucket with a 'tion', 'cean' or 'sion' label on it. Each team must take it in turns to fish in the 'ocean'. If they catch a phoneme that corresponds with their bucket they get to keep the card. If not they must put it back in to the ocean. To make this game a little more exciting you could place shark cards in the ocean and if a child catches a shark they must put all their 'catch' back.

- Play 'Jaws'. Give each child a shark-shaped playing board minus the teeth. Each playing board should have 'tion', 'cean' or 'sion' on it. In a bag put a selection of laminated shark's teeth with a word on each one, but leaving a blank space where the 'tion', 'cean' or 'sion' should be. The children take it in turns to pick a tooth and if it corresponds with their shark they add it to their shark's mouth. If not, they must put it back. At the end of the game shout "Shark Attack!" at which point the children turn over their boards and write all their words on the back. The child who can remember the most words is the winner.

- Play 'Commotion in the Ocean'. Give each child a playing board of an underwater scene with words that have the 'tion', 'cean' or 'sion' graphemes missing. Each child should spin a spinner with 'tion', 'cean' and 'sion' on it as well as a picture of a shark, a jellyfish and some treasure. If the child spins a grapheme they may complete a word on their board containing that grapheme. If they spin the treasure, they may complete any word they like. If they spin a jellyfish they have been stung and lose a word, and if they spin a shark they can 'eat' one of every other player's words! The winner is the child with the most completed words at the end of the game.

Display Ideas

- Paint large pictures of underwater creatures.

- Bubble-print a background using shades of blue. Cut out and collage an underwater scene onto the background.

- Using the poems from the cross-curricular links, enlarge and illustrate the poems.

- Using a variety of collage materials ask the children to create an underwater scene. Focus on the use of different textiles, for example, sand could depict the seabed, green string could depict seaweed, blue cellophane could depict waves etc.

Cross-curricular Links

- **LITERACY** – Look at the use of rhyme in the text and ask the children to write their own rhyming poem about a sea creature.

- **R.E.** – Discuss the importance of animals in Christianity and other religions. Refer to Christian stories such as 'Jonah and the Whale', 'Noah and His Ark' and 'Daniel and the Lion'. Discuss the significance of the animals within the stories.

Mr Men Antonyms

Focus of Learning

- To collect antonyms and discuss differences of meaning and spelling

Whole-class Starter

- Read the story *Mr. Happy* by Roger Hargreaves (Egmont Books Ltd). Talk to the children about similarities and differences between the characters in the story. Explain that the two characters in the story are opposites and that the grown up word for opposites is 'antonym'. Ask the children if they know of any other Mr Men characters and if they have an opposite.

- Make a set of Mr Men picture cards that show opposites. For example, Mr Happy and Mr Sad, Mr Noisy and Mr Quiet, Mr Lazy and Mr Busy, Mr Right and Mr Wrong (you may need to create a selection of your own characters). Place them randomly on the board. Ask the children to match the pairs so that the opposite pairs are next to each other. Discuss why these characters are opposites.

- Play 'Act an Antonym' using the cards from the above activity. Using a large area ask the children to stand in a space (to organise the children into a space you could allocate them each a hoop to stand in). Pull a card out of a box or bag and read it to the children. Ask the children to act out the antonym to the word on the card. For example, if you pull out the word 'fast' the children must act out 'slow'.

Practical Activities

- Play 'Antonym Snap'. Make a set of antonym snap cards, containing pictures and words. Deal the cards amongst the group evenly. Each child takes it in turns to turn a card over and place it in the middle of the table. If a child spots a pair of antonyms they shout out "Snap!" and they win all the cards in the middle of the table. The object is to try and win all the cards.

- Ask the children to make a zigzag antonym book using the Mr Men characters as a stimulus.

- Play 'Antonym Dominoes'. Make a large set of laminated dominoes that relate to different antonyms. Share the dominoes equally amongst the children. The children take it in turns to lay a domino on the table. They must attempt to get rid of all their dominoes by matching the antonyms on the dominoes.

Display Ideas

- In pairs invent Mr Men antonym characters by painting and using collage material.

- Using polystyrene tiles and black and white printing inks, ask the children to create a set of antonym tiles. Arrange the tiles together to create an antonym collage. Ask the children to write the antonyms they can see and add them to the display.

- Ask the children to plan and photograph each other performing opposite still images. Create a class antonym book or use the pictures for display.

Cross-curricular Links

- **LITERACY** – Write a story based on invented antonym characters. Perform to the class as a puppet show.

- **GEOGRAPHY** – Introduce the children to directional language such as 'up', 'down', 'in', 'out', 'left', 'right', 'north', 'south' etc.

Sail Through a Sea of Synonyms

Whole-class Starter

Focus of Learning

- To collect synonyms and discuss differences of meaning and how they may be used to improve their writing

- In role as a confused old sea captain, explain to the children that a boat used to be called just a 'boat', but nowadays it can be called 'ship', 'tanker', 'vessel' etc. Explain that weather reports are difficult to understand because the words keep changing, for example, an iceberg that is big and dangerous was recently described as a 'humongous hazardous iceberg'. Show the children several examples of synonyms, for example, 'big', 'large' and 'colossal', or 'small', 'tiny' and 'minute'. Explain that these words are synonyms. Make a set of synonym cards for each child. The children must find their corresponding words and group them on a board.

- Play 'A Sea of Synonyms'. This game should be played in a large space. Make several sets of synonym cards in the shape of waves, choosing words that have plenty of alternatives. Place the cards face down all over the hall floor. Split the class into six teams and allocate each team a mat to sit on which represents their 'boat'. Give each team a word that corresponds with a set of synonym cards on the floor. A player from each team runs on the sound of a boat horn to a word. If it is a synonym they may take it back to their boat and the next person in their team can run and pick up another word. If it is not a synonym they must choose another word. The winning team is the first team in which every team member has found a synonym and brought it back to their boat.

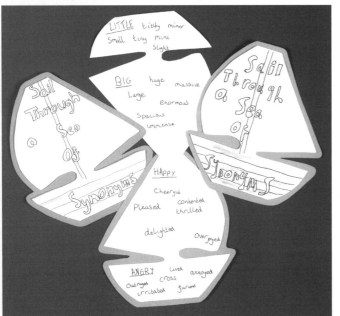

- Play 'Synonym Salute'. Make a set of synonym cards that have several meanings. Ask the children to work in pairs or small groups. Show the children a word. They must write three synonyms that correspond to the word on a whiteboard. The winner is the first team to write the words and shout "Aye-aye captain!" whilst saluting.

Practical Activities

- Play 'Sail the Synonym Sea'. Use an underwater sea mat or create your own giant underwater board game. Make a set of synonym cards. Lay half of them across the underwater sea mat from one side to the other and deal the others out to the players so that each has four cards. Make a 'boat' counter for each player. Each player takes it in turns to roll a dice and move their boat across the synonym cards. If they have a synonym amongst their cards for the card they land on, they may lay it on top. The winner is the person who gets rid of all of their synonym cards first.

- Work with a small group to teach them how to use a thesaurus to find synonyms. Make a set of sentences related to the sea captain, for example, 'Sinbad the sea captain sailed a ship called "Jessie" '. The children must pick a sentence and use the thesaurus to look up an alternative synonym to replace the highlighted word in the sentence.

- Play 'Search for a Synonym'. Make each pair of children a wordsearch containing synonyms. Make a set of corresponding synonym cards on boat shapes. Stick the boat-shaped synonym cards around the school. Send each pair to walk around the school with their laminated wordsearch and a pen. When they find a boat they must find as many corresponding synonyms as they can on their wordsearch. They then look for another boat-shaped synonym card until they have found as many as they can.

Display Ideas

- Paint and collage a giant sea captain.

- Sponge the background of the display to create a sea effect.

- Paint boats with coloured sails.

- Ask children to write large synonym labels to stick on sails and corresponding synonym labels to place in the sea.

- Make crosswords of synonyms.

Cross-curricular Links

- **LITERACY** – Write a synonym story about the sea captain's adventures. Give each child three words and get them to think of as many synonyms as they can. Use these synonyms in their story.

- **GEOGRAPHY** – Identify on a world map various seas and oceans that the sea captain may have visited.

- **SCIENCE** – Floating and sinking: put synonyms on cubes and see how many synonyms each boat will hold before it sinks.

Sshhh it's the Silent Letters!

Whole-class Starter

Focus of Learning

- To investigate words that have silent letters

- Whisper to the children that they have to be quiet because some of the phonemes in the words that you are going to look at today are asleep. Explain that because they are asleep they don't make a sound … they are silent letters! Tell the children that if they wake them up the phonemes will make different sounds and the children won't be able to read the words. Produce a pyjama bag that is full of words that contain silent letters, for example, 'knight', 'write', 'gnome', 'when' etc. Give each child a whiteboard and a pen. Read the word, emphasising the different phonemes, and ask the children to identify and write on their whiteboard which phoneme is sleeping in the word.

- Play 'Sshhh it's Bedtime!' Prepare a selection of words on the interactive whiteboard, some with silent letters and some without. For example, 'Wednesday', 'comb', 'dog' and 'shark'. Reveal one word at a time, if the word contains a silent letter the children should whisper 'Sshhh it's bedtime!' and you drag the word to a picture of a bed and tuck it in!

- Play 'Wake Up, Shake Up'. Make two sets of cards: one set should have words that have a silent letter (pictures may be needed to help children read the words) and the other set should have the corresponding silent letter. Give half of the children a word card each and half of the children a silent letter card each. The children who have a silent letter should 'go to sleep' on the floor and the other children should make a circle around them, holding their cards in front of them. Play some gentle 'bedtime' music and then sound an alarm that will wake up the silent letters. They must run to find the corresponding word for their silent letter. Once partners have been found, the children should practise saying the word with the letter 'awake', pronouncing the silent phoneme. Explain to the children that this is a good way of remembering that the silent letter is there when you are spelling.

Practical Activities

- Play 'Night Night, Sleep Tight'. Make each child a playing board with a picture of a sleepy child on it surrounded by six things they need before they are ready for bed, for example, teddy, book, pyjamas, light etc. Each of these objects should have a word that contains a silent letter. Prepare a spinner or dice with the corresponding silent letters on it. The children must take it in turns to spin the spinner or roll a dice and see if they have a word that has that silent letter in. If they have they may cover it up. The first child to cover all their words is ready for bed and is the winner.

- Ask the children to write words with silent letters, emphasising the silent letter by drawing it really big and adding illustrations such as a nightcap, sleepy eyes and a 'zzzz' speech bubble. Explain to the children that this will help them to remember that the silent letter is there when they are spelling.

- Prepare on the interactive whiteboard a page with silent letters all around the edge. In the centre of the page create a presentation in which a single word will appear and then disappear. Most of the words should have silent letters in them, for example, 'knife' but a few should not such as 'cat'. A child at a time stands in front of the board with a 'word-splatter'. As the words appear on the board the child must decide whether they have a silent letter. If they have a silent letter the child must splat the correct letter from around the edge of the board. Each correct answer wins the child a point.

Display Ideas

- Create a bedtime scene as a background with a person in bed asleep. Cut out large silent letters and display on the bed. Add twinkly lights and stars for a night time effect.

- Display words drawn by the children with the silent letters illustrated.

- Write words with the silent letters missing and replaced by a star with a question mark.

Cross-curricular Links

- **ART** – Create a picture in the style of Van Gogh's Starry Night using thick oil paints.

- **PSHCE** – Read *Peace at Last* by Jill Murphy (Macmillan Children's Books) or *I Am Not Sleepy and I Will Not Go to Bed* by Lauren Child (Hachette Children's Books) and discuss with the children the importance of sleep and their bedtime routines.

One Wobbly Wheelbarrow

Whole-class Starter

- Read the book *One Wobbly Wheelbarrow* by Gwen Pascoe and Darren Pryce (Era Publications). Ask the children what they notice about each of the phrases in the book and explain that when words begin with the same phoneme it is known as 'alliteration'. Make it clear that alliteration is the phoneme at the beginning of the word, not the grapheme; use the phrase "one wobbly wheelbarrow" to highlight this.

- Present the children with their own wobbly wheelbarrow each and explain that you found it at the end of the garden. Pull out one object at a time from your own wobbly wheelbarrow, for example, a gardening glove, an old welly boot, a broken spade etc. Ask the children to work with a partner and give each pair an object from the wheelbarrow. They must think of an alliterative phrase to describe their object. Each pair should share their phrase with the class.

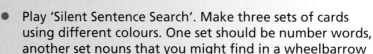

- Play 'Silent Sentence Search'. Make three sets of cards using different colours. One set should be number words, another set nouns that you might find in a wheelbarrow or garden, and the final set alliterative words that correspond with the nouns and numbers. Give each child a card and explain that the idea of the game is to make an alliterative sentence but they must do it in silence! The children must walk around the room and show each other their cards until they find children whose words go with theirs to make an alliterative sentence and then they should sit down. Ask each group to say their sentence in numerical order.

Practical Activities

- Make a wheelbarrow-shaped zigzag book and ask the children to write and illustrate their own version of 'One Wobbly Wheelbarrow' using alliterative phrases.

- Play 'Alliteration All Change'. Make a set of playing cards that include number words, nouns related to things in the garden and adjectives that correspond with the nouns to make alliterative phrases. Deal each child five cards. The children must look at their cards and try and make an alliterative phrase. On a given signal the children all choose one card they would like to swap and pass it to their right. The children look at their cards again and choose another they want to swap. This exercise is repeated until one child has made a complete alliterative phrase and shouts "One wobbly wheelbarrow!"

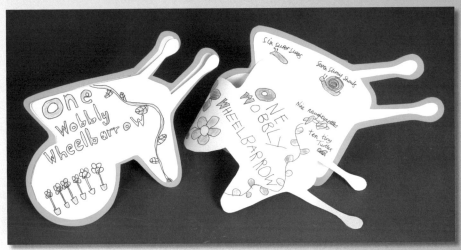

- Make an alliterative alphabet including pictures of things related to the garden and annotate each picture with an alliterative phrase.

Display Ideas

- Paint and collage a giant wheelbarrow.

- Paint, collage and chalk pastel pictures of things that might be found in a wheelbarrow.

- Colour mix shades of green using powder paint and paint leaves for the border of the display.

- Ask the children to write giant-sized alliterative phrases as captions.

- Sew plant and flower pictures for topic book covers.

Cross-curricular Links

- **ART** – Sketch a variety of flowers and plants. Encourage the children to look at detail and use a variety of sketching pencils to add shade and tone.

- **SCIENCE** – Give each small group a wheelbarrow containing a selection of alphabet letters and a whiteboard and pen. Ask them to explore the school grounds in search of things that begin with the letters in their wheelbarrow. When they find an object they must write an alliterative phrase on their whiteboard.

  Classify plants using Venn diagrams and create a question tree about plants.

  Ask the children to make prints of their hands in different shades of green for a 'Greenfingers' display.

- **MATHS** – Work on ordinal numbers and number words.

The Kiss That Missed

Whole-class Starter

- Read the story *The Kiss That Missed* by David Melling (Hodder Children's Books). Ask the children to think where the kiss went and who the kiss met on its journey. Ask the children to work in pairs to write on big strips of paper keywords about the kiss's journey. Stick these on the board. Reread the story and ask the children to identify how the author describes the places, people and animals the kiss meets in the story. For example, 'dribbly wolves', 'smelly wood' and 'happy queen'. Ask them to write their ideas on stick-its and stick them on the relevant keywords. Discuss with the children that each of the words has a double consonant in it. Highlight on the board. Ask the children if they can hear that it is a double consonant. Explain that because two sounds can't be heard each double consonant represents one phoneme.

Focus of Learning

- To investigate and learn to spell words with double consonants

- Play 'Kissing Consonants'. Give each child a laminated golden kiss and a pen. Write keywords from the story on the board. The children have to identify whether it has a double consonant or not. If it has they write the double consonant on their kiss and hold it up. Make the game more difficult by showing the children a picture and saying the word. Begin with fairly easy words that they might know, for example, 'mummy', 'daddy' and 'happy'. Reveal if they are correct by turning over the picture and showing them the word on the back with the double consonant highlighted in gold.

- Play 'Catch Your Consonants'. This game should be played in a large space. Make a set of laminated cards of words with the double consonants omitted. For example, 'h a _ _ y'. Make a set of large laminated cards with the corresponding double consonants on them and attach them onto bibs. Choose children to wear the bibs and stand them in the middle of the allocated area. Give the other children a word card each. On a given signal the children should run and 'catch their double consonant'.

Practical Activities

- Draw, colour and label a 'wanted' poster for a knight. Encourage the children to label the knight using descriptive words that have double consonants, for example, 'He must have a galloping horse', 'He must have a symmetrical shield', 'He must wear shimmering armour' etc.

- Play 'Catch the Kiss That Missed'. Play this game in a large space. You will need a selection of bouncy balls and a fishing net for each child in the group. On each of the balls write or stick either a double consonant or a kiss (x). Stand with your back to the children who each should be holding a net and throw the balls over your head. The children run to catch a ball in their net. If they catch a ball with a double consonant they must write a word that includes that double consonant on their whiteboard. If they catch a kiss they must miss a turn. Repeat with different balls and a different number of kisses each go. The winner is the child with the most double consonant words written correctly on their whiteboard.

- Play 'Double Consonant Bingo'. Make each child a different bingo board with words on each square with their double consonants missing. Make a set of bingo balls with double consonants on them and put them in a bowl. In role as a bingo caller pull a double consonant out of the bowl and tell the children what it is. The children check to see if it corresponds with a word on their bingo board. If it does they cover the missing letters with a counter. The winner is the first child to complete their bingo board and shout "I'm a double consonant winner!"

Display Ideas

- Sponge a background of hills and sky.

- Paint and collage a knight on his horse.

- Paint and collage all the things in the story with double consonants that the kiss meets.

- Ask the children to write captions with the double consonants highlighted in gold.

Cross-curricular Links

- **ART** – Create a clay shield for the knight.

- **LITERACY** – Draw a story map of the journey of the kiss.
  Write a love poem to Happy Harry using double consonants.

- **HISTORY** – Retell and discuss the Legend of King Arthur and the knights of the round table.
  Retell the Legend of George and the dragon.

Powerful Verbs

Whole-class Starter

- In role as a super hero called 'Powerman', tell the children that you are just like any other superhero because you have a superpower. Explain that Superman can fly, Spiderman can make webs and climb walls but you can turn verbs into powerful verbs! Tell the children a normal human being would say, "I went to the shops" but a powerman would say, "I sprinted to the shops" or "I strolled to the shops". Explain to the children what a verb is. Show them a selection of words (include verbs and nouns) and ask the children to sort out the verbs. Discuss their choices.

- Use the verbs that the children have sorted out and show how you can change them into powerful verbs using your superpowers. This could be done effectively on an interactive whiteboard using a multimedia package. Ask the children to say the powerful verbs in superhero voices.

Focus of Learning

- To experiment with changing simple verbs in sentences and discussing their impact on meaning

- Play 'Superhero Sentences'. Show the children a sentence that includes a verb. For example, 'I said "go away" to my brother'. Ask the children to identify the verb in the sentence and ask them to work with a talk partner to change the verb into a powerful verb. The children share their answers and look at different possibilities, for example, 'shouted', 'screamed', 'whispered', 'snarled' etc.

Practical Activities

- Play 'Powerful Pairs'. Make a pairs game either using two different coloured cards or on the interactive whiteboard. One set of cards should be verbs and the other set of cards should be a powerful verb alternative. Children take it in turns to turn over two cards. If the cards match, for example, 'said' and 'shouted', they may keep them. If not they must return them face down. The winner is the player with the most pairs at the end of the game.

- Play 'Power Play'. Make a dice with a verb on each side. Make each player in the group a wordsearch full of powerful verbs that relate to the verbs on the dice. Each player takes it in turns to roll the dice and find a powerful verb that could replace the word on the dice. The person with the most powerful verbs on their wordsearch at the end of the game wins.

- Play 'Super Sentences'. Make a set of Powerman cards with sentences on the reverse that include a verb and place them around the school. Give each child a whiteboard and a pen. The children must walk around the school and find a Powerman picture. They should read the sentence on the reverse and write on their whiteboard a powerful verb that they could use as a substitution for the verb to improve it. The most powerful verb wins! Continue until they have found all the cards.

Display Ideas

- Paint and collage a giant flying Powerman.

- Draw and chalk pastel Powerman in a variety of scenarios and write sentences using powerful verbs to describe what Powerman is doing.

- Ask children to write powerful verbs in a cartoon style. Include verbs so that children can match to the powerful verbs.

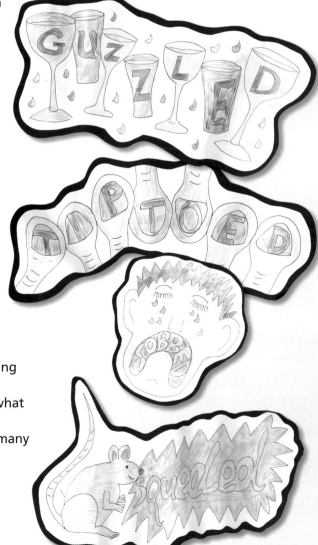

Cross-curricular Links

- **LITERACY** – Write and illustrate a Powerman cartoon strip using powerful verbs.
  Ask children to invent their own superhero, thinking about what superpower they would like to have.
  Ask them to write a story involving their superhero using as many powerful verbs as they can.

- **SCIENCE** – Discuss the fact that verbs can change to powerful verbs. Investigate changing materials.

Mr A and His Friend An

Whole-class Starter

- In role as Mr A accompanied by either a teaching assistant or a pupil who has been briefed called An, tell the children that you are able to stand next to most words in a sentence, however you are terrified of the vowels 'a', 'e', 'i', 'o' and 'u'. Explain that whenever a vowel starts a word your friend An helps you out and stands next to the word instead.

Focus of Learning

- To understand that 'a' precedes a consonant and that 'an' precedes a vowel

- Make a paddle for each child in the class with 'a' on one side and 'an' on the other. Show the children a word and picture and ask them to decide if Mr A can stand next to that word. The children must decide and hold up the appropriate side of the paddle. For example, if the phrase is 'rugby ball' the children would show the 'a' on the paddle, but if it was 'elephant' they would show 'an'. This activity could be prepared on the interactive whiteboard (see page 67).

- Play 'Cat and Mouse'. A large space is needed for this game. Split the class into two groups and ask them to stand next to each other in two long lines. One group are named the 'an' group and the other are the 'a' group. Say a word and if it begins with a vowel the 'a' group must run away and the 'an' group must try and catch them. If you say a word that does not begin with a vowel the 'an' group must run away and the 'a' must try and catch them. If a child is caught they are out the game.

- Show the children the words 'uniform' and 'unicorn' and ask them if Mr A can sit next to these words. Explain that they begin with a vowel so usually the answer would be no, but in this case, because the word is making the long-vowel sound rather than the short-vowel sound, Mr A is not scared of it and can stand next to it.

Practical Activities

- Prepare a piece of text for each child in the group. In the text include lots of mistakes related to the use of 'a' and 'an'. Make a spinner or dice that has the following instructions on: 'correct one mistake', 'correct two mistakes', 'miss a go', 'choose someone else to correct a mistake', 'rub one correction out'. The children take it in turns to spin the spinner and carry out the appropriate instruction. The winner of the game is the first child to find all the mistakes.

- Play 'Active "an" or "a" '. Make a set of cards that have pictures on them. Place the cards around the class or school. The children must work in pairs to find a picture card and decide if it should have 'an' or 'a' in front of it. The children must write a sentence that includes the appropriate 'an' or 'a'. An extension to this activity would be to ask the children to add in an adjective that corresponds with the correct 'a' or 'an' in the sentence, for example, 'an angry ant' or 'a red balloon'.

- Play 'Mr A's Lotto'. Make a set of lotto cards with pictures or words on; some that begin with vowels and some that do not. Make a dice or spinner that has 'a' or 'an' on three sides. The children take it in turns to roll the dice or spin the spinner. If it lands on 'a' the children must identify a picture that begins with a consonant and so should be preceded by an 'a' and vice versa for 'an'. The children could write the correct 'a' or 'an' over the picture or word.

Display Ideas

- Paint and collage a picture of Mr A and An.

- Ask the children to write words and illustrate the initial letter using a picture that corresponds with the word.

- Create a table-top display in which the children can sort a selection of mixed-up objects into the correct hoops, either 'an' or 'a' hoops.

Cross-curricular Links

- **MFL** (Modern Foreign Languages) – Look at the use of 'le' and 'la' to precede words.

- **LITERACY** – Work on vowels and consonants.
  Play 'Word Detectives'. Ask the children to look through books and make a tally chart of how many 'a' and 'an' words they can find.

Harry the Homophone Hippy

Whole-class Starter

- In role as Harry the Homophone Hippy, explain you have discovered that within the English language there are words that sound the same but have different meanings. These words are "really heavy" because although sometimes they are spelled the same, a lot of the time they are spelled differently! Ask the children if they can give any examples. Explain that these words are called 'homophones'.

- Play 'Hilarious Homophones'. On an interactive whiteboard pre-prepare a multi-media presentation that consists of clues that have both homophones in the sentence. For example, 'Two of a fruit = pair and pear', 'Not strong for seven days = weak and week'. Ask the children if they can guess the homophone pairs. Show the children two pictorial clues, one for each homophone, and ask them if they can spell the two words. Discuss the parts of the words that are the same and the parts that are different.

- Play 'Hit the Homophone'. Make a set of large homophone words that can be placed on the board. Include some homophones that are spelled incorrectly, for example, 'knight', 'night', 'nite' and 'niht'. Place all four words on the board. Split the class into two or three teams and sit them behind each other in rows. Give each first person in the team a splatter. Read out a sentence that includes one of the homophone words. For example, "The knight rode his big, white horse". The children must splat the correct word with their splatter. The team who splats first wins a point. Repeat until every team member has had a go.

Practical Activities

● Play 'Hunt the Homophone'. Make a set of star-shaped cards that have a homophone on each. Hide the cards around the school or classroom. Make a board that has two columns; one with 'hidden word' at the top and one with 'homophone word'. The children must search for the hidden homophones. If they find one they write it in the column that says 'hidden homophone' and in the opposite column they must write correctly the other homophone that matches it. Once they have collected all ten pairs of homophones ask the children to put them into a word search and write their own clues for each pair of homophones.

● Play 'Homophone Four in a Row'. Make a set of A4-sized boards that consist of ten by ten square grids. Make a set of small word cards; some with homophones and others without. Each pair of children needs a board and a selection of different coloured counters or whiteboard pens. The children pick a card from a bag or box. If they pick out a homophone card they must say what the matching homophone is and spell it correctly; they can then place a counter or a mark on their board. For example, if a child picks out 'see' they say that the other 'sea' is water that can be swum in and is spelled 's-e-a'. If a child picks a card that is not a homophone or if they can't spell the other homophone correctly, they miss a go. The winner is the child who gets four counters or marks on their board in a row.

● Play 'Have You Got the Homophone?' This game is based on the game of dominoes. Make a set of cards that have sentences with the homophone missing on one side and homophone words on the opposite side. The object of the game is to get rid of all the dominoes by matching the homophone to its appropriate sentence.

● Play 'Homophone Hoops'. Make a grid using large hoops (20 or more). In each hoop place a homophone card face down. Read out a sentence with a missing homophone. One child at a time turns over a homophone card in one of the hoops. If they are correct they keep the card. If not they turn the card back over and you should read another sentence.

Display Ideas

● Draw, paint and collage Harry the Homophone Hippy.

● In pairs ask the children to draw and pastel homophone pairs.

● Ask the children to write sentences that contain a homophone. Instead of writing the homophone ask the children to draw a large flower. Place on the display with the question 'Can you fill in the missing homophone?'

Cross-curricular Links

● **LITERACY** – Ask the children to choose five sets of homophones (ten words in total) and use these words to write a hilarious homophone story.

Make a class homophone dictionary. Each page should include the different version of each word, a definition and an illustrated sentence.

● **ICT** – Ask the children to use a multimedia package to create their own homophone presentation based on Harry the Hippy's homophone presentation.

Tricky Trevor

Whole-class Starter

Focus of Learning
- To learn high frequency or topic words

- Prepare words that relate to the topic the children are studying, for example, they might be studying the Egyptians. In role as Tricky Trevor (a very studious character) explain that there are many tricky words in the English language and you have come to investigate ways to tackle spelling them. Reveal a selection of words and place them on the board. Together the children read them and sort them into words they think are regular and irregular. With the help of the children reveal which words are which. To make this more visual, on the back of each word you could colour code the card. For example, red could equal irregular words and green could equal regular words. Remove all the green words leaving just the red irregular words.

- Explain that the words left are all tricky and you are going to look closely at each word. Reveal an enormous magnifying glass and put one word at a time on the board, for example, 'Egypt'. Ask the children to discuss with a talk partner which part of the word is tricky. Ask them to think about whether there is one or more than one tricky phoneme in the word and to circle the tricky parts. For example, in 'Egypt' they should circle the 'e' and the 'y': 'e' because it makes its long vowel phoneme, and 'y' because it makes an 'i' rather than a 'y' phoneme.

- Repeat the above activity with core words from the topic, for example, 'Egyptian', 'pharaoh', 'sphinx', 'sarcophagus', 'archaeologist', 'pyramid', 'desert', 'tomb', 'death mask', 'cartouche', 'hieroglyphics' and 'ancient'. Discuss with the children how they might tackle spelling these words such as breaking them down into syllables and tackling a syllable at a time, or using mnemonics, for example, ' "i" before "e" except after "c" '. They might relate it to root words, for example, 'Egypt' and 'Egyptian'. In pairs give each group a word and ask them to discuss the tricky part of the word, how they would tackle the word and how they would remember how to spell it in the future. Discuss the results with the whole class.

Practical Activities

- Before you carry out the practical activities explain to the children that at the end of the session there will be a spelling test to check if they can use strategies to help spell tricky words.

- Play 'Pyramid Puzzle'. Make a set of laminated bingo-style boards in the shape of a pyramid. On the board write a selection of tricky words. Make each board different. Make a spinner or a dice with three pictures of Trevor on it, two crosses and one tick. Give each child a board and pen. The children take it in turn to spin the spinner or roll the dice. If it lands on Trevor they must circle a tricky part of one of their words. If they spin a cross they must rub out all their tricky bits and start again. If they spin a tick everybody can circle a tricky part of a word. The object of the game is to cover all the tricky bits in each individual word.

- Play 'Tricky Trail'. In a large space make a simple trail, using benches and tunnels, which the children can follow. Make it creative and fun! All the children start at the same starting point. Ask each child to spell a word. If they are correct they move forward through the trail. If they are incorrect they remain still. On the sound of a hooter the children stop and in order to continue they must spell another tricky word. Continue until all the children have reached the end of the trail.

- Ask the children to make their own A4-sized wordsearch using all of Tricky Trevor's words. The children swap wordsearches with each other and try to find their friends' hidden tricky words.

Display Ideas

- Create a display that includes Tricky Trevor and is related to the subject the children are learning about. For example, ask the children to draw or paint several pictures of Trevor with his magnifying glass. Hide Trevor amongst the display background. Paint large pyramids and palm trees for Trevor to hide behind.

- Ask the children to write a selection of words. Highlight the tricky part of the word by backing it on a vibrant colour.

- Make a selection of typed tricky words that are backed on a theme-shaped piece of paper. For example, if studying Egypt you could back them on pyramids. Place them around the room so that children can use them as a reference point throughout their topic.

- Make pyramid maths puzzles and pyramid facts to link with cross-curricular work.

Cross-curricular Links

These activities could be adapted to suit the subject you are learning about. We have linked it to the Ancient Egyptians.

- **ART** – Spell tricky words using hieroglyphics. Display on a cartouche-shaped piece of card.

- **LITERACY** – Make a Tricky Trevor dictionary with words that are tricky to spell.

  Make a Tricky Trevor glossary with words and their meanings.

- **DESIGN & TECHNOLOGY** – Make a 3D pyramid and write Tricky Trevor words on the pyramid. Use it as a teaching aid during lesson time.

- **MATHS** – Make a large set of pyramids that contain number puzzles. The children must try and complete the missing numbers. The bottom numbers on the pyramids when added together make the top number. Challenge the children to create their own pyramid puzzles.

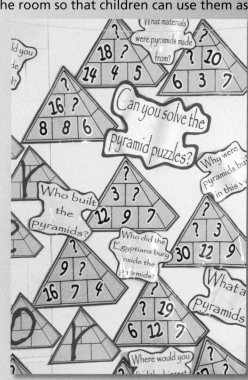

Mr A and His Friend An (page 66)